ESSAYS ON FAITH
CULTURE, AND PHILOSOPHY

Andrew J. Schatkin

University Press of America,® Inc.
Lanham · Boulder · New York · Toronto · Plymouth, UK

Copyright © 2016 by
University Press of America,® Inc.
4501 Forbes Boulevard
Suite 200
Lanham, Maryland 20706
UPA Acquisitions Department (301) 459-3366

Unit A, Whitacre Mews, 26-34 Stannary Street,
London SE11 4AB, United Kingdom

Library of Congress Control Number: 2016933012
ISBN: 978-0-7618-6749-4 (paperback : alk. paper)
eISBN: 978-0-7618-6750-0

Table of Contents

Section II – Essays on Politics. Culture. and Philosophy

Preface

In my previous book, entitled *Essays on the Christian Worldview and Others,* in a series of essays and articles, I discussed my thoughts in various areas including some general areas such as "Why I Believe in Democracy" and "Why I Am against Abortion." In another section of that book I discussed in a series of essays what I think are the elements of the Christian Worldview and, in Section III, I discussed certain political and legal issues that I think important. The book ends with Section IV, a series of literary and philosophical essays.

In this new book, in which it is my great hope that the general public will find something of value and something to think about, I speak about a number of things. For example, I discuss what I think is the meaning of the sacraments in the church, specifically Baptism and Holy Communion, which I see as an encounter with Christ. I take note that the church in the west may be declining in the face of the secular society but is re-emerging in other parts of the world such as Africa and China.

I also explain why I think the Catholic Church opposes contraception. I talk about two things I consider important, namely the relationship between Christ and the present culture, and I posit in this essay that the Church and Christ are somewhat in opposition to the secular culture and should not be informed by the secular culture, but rather should inform and enlighten the secular culture.

I also talk about Satan and his role and note that, although many people see him as a comic figure, he is an integral element and figure in the Christian dogmatic system.

In the second section of his book, which is entitled "Essays on Society and Culture," I note the decline of the American middle class and offer reasons. I also speak about our culture's being totally obsessed and informed by money and that other values should have input. I also discuss that intellectual work and mental work have a greater value than physical work.

I discuss that perhaps the so-called elite in our society are misnamed because of their economic status and power and that perhaps the true elite may be found elsewhere. I also note that Karl Marx may have had some points to make and that there is a failure in American culture, which is based on materialism alone and celebrity status.

Again, it is my hope that this book of essays will serve to stimulate and engage and provoke those who read them. I welcome responses and discussions to any point I have raised in this book and hope, again, that this book will raise significant issues and concepts that will serve to elevate and raise the thoughts and value system or our present society.

Section One

Essays on Faith

Section One – Essays on Faith
Introduction

Some of these essays in this section have been discussed in the general introduction to this book. I do say here, however, that for me these essays point out certain significant issues within the Christian dogmatic system of thought. For example, I note that perhaps the prizes that are given out in our society to the so-called top people perhaps should be given to more humble and serving people. I analyze also that in the Christian faith, there is no opposition to the flesh and that, in fact, Jesus took human form and died the death of a human being.

I also note that Jesus had a very positive relationship with many women who followed him in his ministry and more significantly was born of a woman. I also critique the idea of spirituality as some sort of a vague belief system and note that Christianity concerns Christ, his ministry, and the things he said. Ultimately he offers us eternal life so to define Christianity with the word "spirituality" is a misnomer. I also speak about Jesus' use of the term "Son of God" and "Son of Man" in reference to himself. Through these he serves to connect us with his being fully human and not some sort of spiritual guest from heaven.

These essays, it is my hope and desire, will point the reader to what I think is important and should be understood as a Christian. In fact, I welcome all person of all religions to read these essays in this section and to comment on them.

Chapter 1
A Word about St. Paul

A few months ago, I was watching television and I flicked on a panel discussion about St. Paul and the New Testament. The panel consisted of biblical scholars, mostly representing the more liberal Protestant denominations, which often, I think, reject the historicity of the bible stories and often refer to them as myths. In this little essay, I do not attempt to argue with that perspective, although I disagree with it, but I would like to talk about one particular comment of one of the scholars on the panel.

In Acts, Chapter 9, it is related that Saul, who formerly had been persecuting the new founded church and Christians, went to the high Priest and asked for letters to the synagogues at Damascus to apprehend Christians. It is related in Chapter 9 that as Saul journeyed, a light from heaven flashed about him, and Saul fell to the ground and heard a voice saying to him, "Saul, why do you persecute me?" Saul is related to have said, "Who are you Lord," and the voice that he heard is supposed to have said, "I am Jesus, whom you are persecuting; but rise and enter the city and you will be told what you are to do."

The men who were traveling with Saul were said to have been speechless, hearing a voice, but seeing no one. Saul is said to have risen to the ground and when he opened his eyes, could see nothing and they led him by the hand into Damascus. For three days Saul was without sight and neither ate nor drank. Thereafter, it is related that one Ananias is said to have told Saul, "Jesus appeared to you on the road by which you came and has sent me so that you can regain your sight and be filled with the Holy Spirit." At that point, it is related that the scales fell from Saul's eyes and he regained his sight (Acts, 9: 1–19).

One of the scholars in that panel discussion was of the opinion that Paul's experience on the road to Damascus and his vision resulted from suffering from epilepsy or a mental illness. First, there is no factual evidence as to that opinion, but more important, I think it completely erroneous and wrong. Anyone who has read Paul's letters, which are in the canon of the New Testament, can see that they reveal an outstanding thinker. Paul wrote letters to the Church in Rome; the Church in Corinth; the Church in Galatia; the Church in Philippi; the Church in Thessalonica; and the Church in Ephesus. There are individual letters to a runaway slave, Philemon, and to two individuals, Timothy and Titus. These letters are extremely profound in their presentation and thought and hardly the work of an insane person or an epileptic. These letters have convinced for 2000 years individuals of all races and backgrounds to become Christians.

St. Paul made many missionary journeys throughout Asia Minor and Greece. He went to Greece; Corinth, Antioch and Asia Minor; as well as Ephesus. He is also represented as going to Jerusalem, Miletus, and Caesarea. In fact, St. Paul traveled throughout almost the entire known Graeco-Roman world as an Evangelist. It begs the question to say that a person who could move world history as did St. Paul was mentally handicapped or epileptic. I am not convinced that a person of such intellectual depth, as revealed in his letters, and of such commitment to an idea and person, was insane. If that were the case, for some 2000 years the writings of a purportedly insane man, someone who saw false visions because of his handicap, have brought and continue to bring the world to its feet.

Let me add this final point. If the vision that Saul, or later Paul, saw of risen Christ on the road to Damascus was the product of epilepsy or mental illness, I put forth here Chapter 13 of Paul's letter to the Corinthian Church.

> 1 If I speak in the tongues of men and of angels, but have not love, I am a noisy gong or a clanging cymbals. 2 And if I have prophetic powers, and understand all mysteries and all knowledge, and if I have all faith, so as to move mountains, but have not love, I am nothing. 3 If I give away all I have, and if I deliver my body to be burned, but have not love, I gain nothing.
>
> 4 Love is patient and kind; love is not jealous or boastful; 5 it is not arrogant or rude. Love does not insist on its own way; it is not irritable or resentful; 6 it does not rejoice at wrong, but rejoices in the right. 7 Love bears all things, believes all things, hopes all things, endures all things.
>
> 8 Love never ends; as for prophecies, they will pass away; as for tongues, they will cease; as for knowledge, it will pass away. 9 For our knowledge is imperfect and our prophecy is imperfect; 10 but when the perfect comes, the imperfect will pass away. 11 When I was a child, I spoke like a child, I thought like a child, I reasoned like a child; when I became a man, I gave up childish ways. 12 For now we see in a mirror dimly, but then faced to face. Now I know in part; then I shall understand fully, even as I have been fully understood. 13 So faith, hope, love abide, these three; but the greatest of these is love.

The man who wrote these sentences and produced this thought and who had the vision on the road to Damascus was far from epileptic or mentally ill. These thoughts that I just have put here, if they were the thought of an epileptic or a mental case, have affected more people than most books that have ever been written.

Chapter 2
A Word on the Sacraments

To the outside observer, the Sacraments, whether in the Roman Catholic Church or the Protestant Church, are something of an enigma. In the Catholic Church, there are seven Sacraments: 1) the Eucharist or the Lord's Supper 2) Baptism 3) Marriage 4) Priestly Ordination 5) Confirmation 6) Penance and 7) Last Rites. In the Protestant Church, and in particular in the Lutheran Church, of which I am a member, there are two sacraments: 1) Baptism and 2) the Lord's Supper, or Communion. As I said, for a want of a better word, in the secular or non-Christian world, these sacraments are either misunderstood or seen as irrelevant or as the product of some outmoded, antique world view.

This little essay proposes to explain a bit of the meaning and nature of the two sacraments in the Protestant Church and, in particular, the Lutheran Church. Baptism is an attempt by the Church, as the agent of Christ, to bring a child into relationship with Christ. Baptism is the beginning point of the transformation of an individual into the image of Christ. In a sense, Baptism is an attempt to attach the human soul, and infant soul at that stage of life, to the person of Jesus, who, for the Christian believer, resides in heaven with the other two persons of the Holy Trinity, God the Father and the Holy Spirit. The persons of the Trinity are, so to speak, in Communion or relationship. The relationship is one of love. Baptism brings the infant into a beginning point in a relationship with Christ which will gradually transform or transport him or her to the fullness and riches of what a human being is meant to be.

I would also like to comment on the Communion or Lord's Supper in the Lutheran Church. For many people outside the Church, and outside the Christian belief system, the act of eating the body and blood of a God, in this case Christ, is completely primitive and out of sync with the modem world. The Communion meal involves the element of sacrifice, namely, the death of Christ on the cross to atone for our sins and redeem the human race from its sinfulness and degradation.

As I said, to the outside observer who is more intent with getting an upscale car or a beautiful wife, the sacrifice of Christ, or the reenactment of that sacrifice in the Communion meal, is irrelevant and probably thought of as slightly ridiculous. The outside observer, or better put, modern person, may see participating in the consumption of a God, in this case Christ, as extremely primitive. In some sense, these individuals in this mode of thinking and expression have a point. The consumption, even symbolically or morally, of a God's body and blood is certainly greatly removed from the modern world view. So, quite understandably, these non-Christians see this ceremony as outmoded, irrelevant, and a leftover and legacy of the ancient world in which people had no control over nature and sought by sacrifice, whether of animals or persons, and by consuming that sacrifice as a way of guaranteeing their future in a world whose forces they could not control.

For the Christian, however, the Lord's Supper, for instance, has a different significance. For the Christian, the death of Christ on the cross is the final and ultimate sacrifice, meant to bring a broken and twisted humanity into a fruitful and positive relationship with the Creator and his only begotten Son, Jesus Christ. More important, when a Christian partakes in the Lord's Supper or Communion, once again, the Christian is attaching himself and being transformed into the image of Christ. Or, better put, the Lord's Supper or Communion, brings the Christian believer into relationship with Jesus and into transformation into the image of Jesus, to the personhood and humanity which we all have the potential to be.

In short, the sacraments of Baptism and the Lord's Supper bring the Christian into closer and closer relationship with Jesus. As a result, the person in that relationship is transformed over his or her lifetime into the ultimate and perfected humanity that we, all human beings, were meant to be and can only be in relationship with Jesus and in the course of that relationship become transformed into something we can hardly imagine we could possibly be. I think that this is what Jesus means by our becoming his sons or daughters. Jesus means that, in relationship with him, we grow into his image and likeness, or better put, we are raised up into the humanity that he represents and wishes us to become.

At the present time, it is quite obvious to any thinking person that the human race is failed and broken. The evil and sin that infects the world dominates it. Nevertheless, in Baptism and the Lord's Supper, Jesus still sees humanity as having the capacity to grow into something else and out of the diseased world that the human race has infected and destroyed and now, in its present form, exists as a result of sin, and the fall of mankind into sin. I suppose that all of us must see it as something of a mystery that God would sacrifice his only begotten Son for humanity and for a human race that appears so entirely worthless. It is evidence of the extraordinary love that God possesses for the world that he would trouble himself to die for us and in Baptism and the Lord's Supper still seek us out to transform us into something worthwhile.

Chapter 3
A Word about the Body and the Flesh

There is a misconception that the Christian faith is opposed to physicality and, for want of a better word, the body or the flesh, or perhaps better put, is against sex. To be sure, there is something of an emphasis on virginity, since Christ was born of a virgin, and since then various religious orders have been organized at least in the Orthodox Church and the Roman Catholic Church involving vows of celibacy, poverty, and obedience. There is, it would appear, an anti-sexuality element in the Christian religion. This is emphasized by the fact that there is a common idea that when we die we will be flitting about like some sort of invisible ghosts in some sort of metaphysical world.

Unfortunately, these ideas, which have become attached and involved with the Christian religion, are erroneous. They are erroneous on two grounds. Number one involves the doctrine of the Incarnation. This doctrine posits that Christ was pre-existing and took on human flesh combined with his Godly being in the person of Jesus of Nazareth. In fact, there can be no more affirmation of bodily humanity and sexuality. This doctrine puts an end to any doubts on the subject. The Christian God so affirmed the body, the flesh, and sexual feelings that God took it upon himself to become a full human being with all the attendant feelings I have just referred to. I can think of no other religion in which any God chose to take on human flesh and thereby affirm humanity, bodily being, and of course, sexuality. Only an extremely limited person would say that Jesus had no sexual feelings, since he was fully human.

The second argument against the otherworldly character of Christianity which has been bandied about with the emphasis on virginity and celibacy in certain religious communions of the body of Christ is that Christianity holds that

Christ rose from the dead with a body. He did not come out of the grave like some sort of ghost or spirit, but came out with some sort of body. Once again, we are faced with the glaring fact that the risen Christ has a body and, in fact, ascended into heaven with a body. Once again, the misconception that Christianity is an otherworldly, anti-flesh, anti-physicality religion is belied by this significant historical event and doctrine.

Finally, there is the fact that Christians believe that at some point we will be given the chance to rise again. The Apostle's Creed describes this belief as a belief in the resurrection of the body. Once again, the resurrection of the body as a doctrine and dogma posits not that we will come out of the grave like some sort of flitting ghost or see-through entity, but with a body, in fact, our own body in life.

In sum, this little essay, I think, has cleared up certain misconceptions about the Christian faith that are articulated by those who neither know, understand, or care to understand these doctrines. There is no religion that better affirms physical being, the flesh, humanity, and sexuality than the Christian religion. God created physical beings, men and women. He himself affirmed that creation by taking on human flesh with all its limitations, feelings, and senses. The Christian religion believes that Jesus Christ rose from the dead with a body and presently occupies a body in heaven. The Christian religion articulates the dogma that we will rise from the dead, not as spirits, but with the bodies contiguous and connected with the bodies we had in life. To the best of my knowledge, I can think of no other religion that affirms the flesh more than the Christian religion.

Finally I would add as a little note here that Christianity always has raised and always will raise the status of women in society. Christ was born of a woman, many of his followers were women, and the Genesis account of creation presents males and females with equal amounts of sexual feelings. God, who is spirit, wishes to have a relationship with human beings with bodies and bodily feelings. The Christian religion, in short, far from being an otherworldly, outer space religion, is instead a religion very much of the flesh, the time and the being.

Chapter 4
Who Gets the Prize?

In the past few years, two significant government and political figures have received the Nobel Peace Prize. They are President Barack Obama and former Vice President Al Gore. Who am I to question the judgment of the Nobel Committee or the entitlement or worthiness of these individuals to have been given and to have accepted this great honor? One may wonder that with six billion people on the planet, less prominent political figures might be considered for this honor, figures who might be equally or possibly more worthy of this honor, but lack power and wealth.

I have a comment to make. The other day I read in the *New York Times* a very short story that ten (10) committed Christians from the United States, who had gone to Afghanistan to provide free medical care to those persons in dire poverty, had been murdered. The secular press gave little notice to this event and, in fact, no one I know had much to say about it. Those individuals went to Afghanistan, motivated by the eternal love and mercy of Jesus Christ and his particular concern for the poverty stricken in this world, to carry out his mission with respect to these deeply deprived persons in Afghanistan.

They came from what many people would look down on in certain sections of society, fundamentalist churches in this country. They gave up their lives in sacrifice and love to others. They passed unrecognized and gained no prize or honor. The entire world failed to recognize their supreme sacrifice, which they did by reason of their deeply held faith that God gave his only begotten son to die for all men and women, not because of their worth but because of his love for all humanity, regardless of sex, race, and in particular, economic status.

The media and the world in general had little to say about this event. It has much to say about politicians with a degree of wealth and power and, it would appear, recognizes them and confers upon them prizes. It gives no prize to these Christian people that gave up their lives in love of others.

The Salvation Army, a Protestant sect for over 100 years, has gone into the most economically deprived areas in the cities and the world and given help and aid to the poorest of the poor. They continue to do so. The secular press and the media say nothing about these people's profound commitment to the love of Jesus Christ for all humanity. The media speak much of prominent political figures, rock stars, and in general, people with material status in our society. It has little to say of those Christians presently in their graves in Afghanistan and certainly has had nothing to say about the Salvation Army and its work for the poorest of the poor in the slums of this world.

The media and the press in the West, both North America and Europe, and possibly in Asia and Africa, have little or nothing to say about these people. It would appear to me that there is some discontinuity or disfigurement in our social and political fabric that only politicians get the prize and those Christians who commit their lives to the most deprived in our world are not spoken of. The world, the press, and the media have nothing to say of their work and their deaths. Who should get the prize? One may also ask where true greatness lies.

Chapter 5
The Church Re-emerges

When I was a young man in the 1960s and early 1970s, it was bandied about and was fashionable to say that "God is dead." At one time, as a response to this saying, I saw buttons that read "God is not dead; he is alive and well in Mexico City." Times have greatly altered and, in fact, religion, so to speak, has made a comeback and has even in the United States gained some power that it formerly lacked. Specifically, with the election of Jimmy Carter, who pronounced himself a born-again Christian, Christian belief in the United States in its conservative Protestant form has gained some acceptance. Further, with the election of Ronald Reagan, Evangelical Christianity allied itself with the Republican Party on certain social issues, specifically abortion and homosexuality.

Since that time however, many people have identified themselves as atheists. This is certainly true in Europe, which has become significantly secular and non-Christian in its society and outlook. This development has also been advancing in the United States, with the culture's great emphasis on material possessions and wealth as a measurement and criterion and measuring stick of worth and value for many people. Secularist, agnostic, and atheistic beliefs are held by many people, particularly in the fairly educated, wealthier classes of society in the West.

It would appear that Christian belief has a greater appeal to the poor and less to those with some material wealth. One can conclude that the reason for this is that when one has some sum of money, he or she is less dependent on religious belief and faith, since wealth creates some degree of spiritual independence.

Nevertheless, at least for the better educated, upper middle class people, for most of the Western world, religion, Christianity, and most significantly, the person of Jesus Christ and his message, have become irrelevant and unacceptable. I have heard one colleague of mine, a lawyer, say that religious belief and dogma are fairytales. Many young people I meet have pronounced themselves to me to be atheists.

The church, and specifically, the person and claim of Jesus Christ to be the Son of God—or better put connected to God—and his promise that those who accept him will have eternal life, is irrelevant to many people in the Western world.

It is, however, a fact that the Church and Jesus Christ continue to re-emerge and reinvent themselves in the world. For 60 years, the Church was suppressed in Russia. It has re-emerged there today and many people attend religious functions in the Orthodox Church, as well as in Catholic and Protestant churches. For every declining mainline church in the West, there emerges, in the inner city slums of the United States, street churches. For every non-believing Westerner, there is an African who is daily being baptized by a missionary. I once knew a Jesuit Priest from Nigeria who told me that he went into the countryside in Nigeria baptizing over 100 people a day.

The church is experiencing enormous growth in Africa, Asia, and South America. For every clever secular wealthy Westerner who laughs and mocks at the claim of Jesus of Nazareth and his promise of eternal life and freedom from sin for those who believe in him, there occur in societies other than the West all over the world, every day, a church being built, a Christian community meeting, and new forms of Christian belief emerging.

What can one say about this and about Jesus? Much as the elite laugh at the claims of Jesus Christ, he continues to re-emerge everywhere and in every place. One can conclude that much as the world would like to discount Jesus Christ as the Savior and Redeemer of the world and all humanity, he cannot be suppressed, but will be found in other places, and at other times, in different, and new, and reinvented ways

Chapter 6
A Word on Kingship

The idea or notion of being a king, having a kingdom, and, in a word, kingship in the Bible presents two pictures or two varying concepts as to what constitutes having a kingdom and being a king. In the Hebrew Bible, or the Old Testament, many things are said about what it is to have a kingdom and be a king. For example, in the Book of First Kings, chapter 2, verse 12, it is said that Solomon sat upon the throne of David and his kingdom was firmly established, and in verse 46 it is said that his kingdom was established in the hand on Solomon. What we may gather from these few words is that being a king and having a kingdom in the Hebrew Bible was an accession to power.

In First Chronicles, chapter 14, verse 2, it is said that David was established by the Lord as King over Israel and that his kingdom was highly exalted. In First Chronicles, chapter 17, verse 11, again it is said that the Jewish kingdom will be established. In the book of Esther, chapter 1, verse 4, the King Ashasuerus is represented as showing the riches of his royal glory and splendor and pomp of his majesty for many days: 180 in all. In Psalm 145, verse 11, the Psalmist says that the saints shall speak of the glory of his kingdom and tell of his power and goes on to say in verse 12 of that same psalm that it will be made known to the sons of men the mighty deeds and the glorious splendor of the Lord's kingdom, described in verse 13 as an "everlasting kingdom."

In the Hebrew Bible, the notion of kingship and having a kingdom is connected with riches, glory, and power. On the other hand, Jesus, in the New Testament, presents a different view of kingship and having a kingdom. In Matthew, chapter 21, Jesus is presented as a King nearing Jerusalem, but comes with humility and mounted on a donkey. The crowd surrounding Jesus, who appears in what may be described as hardly the appearance of a King, nevertheless spread their garments before him on the road and cut branches from the trees and spread them on the road. In Mark, chapter 11, again Jesus appears before the crowd as he nears Jerusalem on a donkey. In Luke, chapter 19, again, Jesus comes in humility to Jerusalem and, nevertheless, he is proclaimed as a King.

What conclusion can we draw from this comparison I have presented in this essay on the concept of kingship as presented in the Hebrew Bible and re-presented in the New Testament? It is obvious and well known that the Hebrew Bible presents many instances and sayings about helping the poor and the widows who suffer in that society. Nevertheless, it may be said, that the idea of a King in the Hebrew Bible differs from the presentation of Kingship that Jesus presents to the world in the New Testament. Jesus says to the world that being a King is to come in humility and service. For the world of that time—and this time—being a King is having power, riches, and importance. For the Christian, being a King is humility and using power and riches in the service of others.

The world will always reject the son of God whose kingdom is not material wealth and power, but service, love, and humility. The forces of the world may reject the Kingdom of Jesus, but it remains to be seen whose kingdom will be established and whose will not. Many kings and dictators have risen and fallen. Their reign and power was temporary. The kingship of Jesus founded on humility and service, despite attempts to disestablish it, nevertheless, for some 2,000 years, has attracted adherents, both rich and poor, educated and uneducated. It remains to be seen where the truth will be found and who will find it and who will be King and reign, and who will not.

0

Chapter 7
Galileo: A Thought Misconception

In the 16th century, Galileo, one of the world's greatest scientists and thinkers, ran into a bit of a problem with the Roman Catholic Church and, specifically, the Vatican authorities at that time. It had been formerly thought that the earth was the center of the universe. This misconception emanated from Copernicus. In fact, it is a rather reasonable assumption and is no more ridiculous in a sense than the conception that the earth is flat, since the earth appears to be flat.

Galileo was arrested and accusations were lodged against him by the religious authorities and he was virtually imprisoned for some period of time. I think the Catholic Church, and their position that the earth was the center of the universe, and Galileo in his view that the earth revolved around the sun were both right, but came at the thought from different angles and different perspectives. There is no doubt that the earth revolves around the sun. But in many ways, the earth is the center of the universe, at least theologically, philosophically, and metaphysically. It appears to be the case, despite valiant attempts by scientists to prove otherwise, that human beings have not been found anywhere else in the entire universe. Searches have been made for life, at least in the planets near by us such as Mars and Venus, and nothing has been found. Thus, in a very real sense, for whatever unknown reason, humanity has made its stand on the earth and no other place. No one knows the reason for this, and there appears to be some mystery in connection with this fact and phenomenon.

Humanity, in a very real sense, is the center of things, since everywhere else we look we find nothing resembling life or human beings. The biblical view that the earth is the center of things is true. Thus, the opinion of Galileo is a physical opinion alone. The conclusion of Galileo was a statement of fact. When we know that everywhere we look in the heavens, we find nothing but darkness and void, and on earth alone, life and humanity have developed, we have the absolute confirmation of the Genesis story in Chapter 1 that God created the heavens and the earth. The problem at the time of the controversy of the church with Galileo is that both agreed, but neither understood how both agreed. The Roman Catholic Church felt threatened in its theological stance, but in reality was not, by the conclusion of Galileo that the earth revolved around the sun. There was no challenge there, but merely an observation of fact that failed to change the reality of what is going on, namely, that it is only here on earth that we find humanity.

I am confident that it is here that whatever happens to the human race as time and history move on will take place, and that God in his mercy and grace will move history, as he chooses, for whatever end he wishes to bring about for us all, in whatever process he chooses to employ. The heavens will be there, but humanity and the earth alone will move to whatever inevitable conclusion is ordained. The earth may revolve around the sun, but in this pinprick of life we call earth, there is something going on and, as it occurs and moves along, will bring an end that none of us at the present time understand or know. It is the absolute truth that humanity and earth are the center of things. Galileo was not wrong, nor was the church. Both engaged in a misunderstanding and both were right.

Chapter 8
Rich and Poor: Poverty and Riches

The question of wealth, riches and, in contrast, poverty is addressed in many passages in both the Hebrew Bible and the New Testament. Varying views may be found in both of those documents or, better put, books. The Old Testament, or Hebrew Bible, often speaks of wealth and riches. For example, in 1st Samuel, chapter 17, verse 25, there is a statement that the King will enrich one of his subjects with great riches. In 1st Chronicles, chapter 29, verse 12, there is a statement that riches and honor come from the Lord. In 2nd Chronicles, chapter 1, verse 12, God states to King Solomon that he will give him riches, possessions, and honor. In 2nd Chronicles, chapter 32, verse 27, it is said that King Hezekiah had very great riches and honor and made for himself treasuries for silver, for gold, and for precious stones. In 2nd Chronicles, chapter 18, verse 1, there is a statement that King Jehosaphat had great riches and honor.

There are many statements in the books of Psalms and Proverbs connected with God's granting wealth to those who believe in him and follow his commandments. Psalm 112, verse 3 says that wealth and riches are in the house of the man who fears the Lord. Proverbs 19, verse 14 states that house and wealth are inherited from fathers. Proverbs chapter 8, verse 18 says riches and honor are with me, enduring wealth and prosperity. There is a further statement in verses 20 and 21 of that same chapter that, "I walk in the way of righteousness, the paths of justice, endowing with wealth those who love me and filling their treasuries."

On the other hand, the Hebrew Bible contains many admonitions and statements concerning the commandment to assist the poor. These statements are often found in the Book of Psalms. For example in Psalm 113, verse 7, there is a statement that the Lord raises the poor from the dust, lifts the needy from the ash heap, and makes them sit with the princes of his people. In Psalm 82, verse 3, it is said that God gives justice to the weak, fatherless, afflicted, and needy and delivers them from the hand of the wicked. In Psalm 72, verse 13, there is the statement that God has pity on the weak and needy and saves the lives of the needy. There are many examples of the concern of the Jewish culture, as reflected in the Hebrew Bible, for the needy and equal condemnation for those who do not help the poor. For further examples of this concern for the poor in the Hebrew Bible the following passages from the Book of Psalms are useful and enlightening. Psalm 12, verse 5; Psalm 40, verse 17; Psalm 69, verse 33.

It is clear that there are two strands concerning riches and poverty, or better put the rich and poor, in the Hebrew Bible. It is quite clear that there is a strand of thought in Jewish culture at that time that God blesses with riches his people who follow his edicts and commandments. Parallel with that thought, manifested in Jewish culture, is a very distinct and explicit concern for the poor and needy. I will say this much on this particular issue concerning the status and importance of wealth and riches in Jewish culture in the Hebrew Bible and the parallel concern for the poor and needy, that although there is an apparent concern in the Jewish culture at that time for the poor and needy in the Hebrew Bible, nevertheless poverty itself is not a goal or a manifestation of God's favor within the Jewish culture in the Hebrew Bible.

On the other hand, in the New Testament, poverty and the poor have a special and distinct place in the Christian worldview. Jesus says in the Beatitudes in Matthew, chapter 5, verse 3, that not only are the poor in spirit blessed, but theirs is the kingdom of heaven. In Matthew, chapter 11, verse 5, there is a statement that the poor have good news preached to them. In Matthew, chapter 19, verse 21, the rich young man is told by Jesus that if he wishes to have eternal life or be perfect, he should go and sell what he possesses and give to the poor. It is recorded in verse 22 that when the young man heard this, he went away sorrowful, for he had great possessions. In Luke, chapter 6, verse 20, Jesus states that the poor are blessed and that theirs is the Kingdom of God. In Luke, chapter 14, verse 13, Jesus says that when you give a feast, invite the poor, the maimed, the lame, and the blind and that you will be blessed because they cannot repay you. In Luke, chapter 14, verse 21, in a parable, Jesus says again that the poor are to be brought in from the streets and the lanes of the city to the banquet along with the lame, blind, maimed. Again in Luke, chapter 18, verse 22, Jesus again tells a young man to sell all he has and distribute to the poor and follow him. In Luke, chapter 19, verse 8, Jesus tells Zacchaeus that salvation has come to him because he has said he will give half of his goods to the poor and restore fourfold anyone he has defrauded.

What we may conclude about poverty and poor in the Christian manifestation is that in the Christian system poverty and being poor is a goal. There is a distinct thought trend and thrust in the mind and thought of Jesus and his sayings in the Gospels that poverty and giving away our wealth raises us up spiritually and brings us to a superior and elevated position in the eternal scheme. Along with the statements of Jesus that the last shall be first, and that what you do to the least you do unto me. Christianity. although recognizing our duties to the poor, is a thought system that elevates poverty and the poor in some sense to an actually higher position than the rich and powerful occupy in the temporal world. One can only guess the reason for this, but one can say that poverty, along with suffering, raises us up in some sense as human beings. Wealth and riches, in the same way, bring us down or, rather, cut us off from the truth of it all, that we are all on borrowed time and that whatever wealth we may have will not change our dependent status as creatures and our ultimate mortality.

Chapter 9
Jesus the Litigator

I've been a New York-area lawyer for more than 30 years, but I also received a Master of Divinity from Princeton Theological Seminary in 1973. My theological studies intensified my desire to help make the world a more just and equal place. The practice of law gave me the means to do so. Today, I see a strangely distorted and mean-spirited view of Christianity dominating the media.

Jesus of Nazareth, or Jesus Christ, continues to intrigue all sectors of society, all peoples, all races, both rich, not so rich and, most particularly the underclass and poor. In an age that emphasizes money, materialism, outright greed, and admiration for the rich and powerful, he offers an alternative.

Yet Jesus is an enigmatic and troubling figure. For many people in the world, he is seen as a kind of general love figure, the ultimate nice guy. After all, that's what the world wants to see in other people—niceness, tolerance, humanity, and kindness. Far from being solely concerned with being loving and nice to people, however, Jesus is the ultimate litigator. One might see him as an advocate of the underclass. Perhaps one could see Jesus as a socialist or communist, since in the gospels he seems to make a point of associating with and advocating for the poor and working class.

Jesus is the beginning point of advocating a new world system without class, economic, race, or sex divisions. Jesus is the ultimate litigator. But his litigation is for the poverty-stricken and the underclass. Jesus was himself a working man, a carpenter, and he spent his entire life with working people or even less. He himself walked about with a group of working men, one a tax collector, and some fishermen, working miracles and making observations to the working class for the most part. Jesus is criticized as consorting with undesirable people, or better put, tax collectors and sinners. Perhaps today, Jesus might be seen as a labor organizer or a community organizer, opposing the forces of government and wealth.

Jesus did not respect or admire wealth or power. Quite to the contrary, he says the poor or humble—the poor in spirit—are blessed, and that in future years, they will be the ruling class, replacing the present oligarchs and plutocrats. Jesus approached Jerusalem as a king, but rode on a donkey with a somewhat disheveled appearance before the crowds. He was tried and executed as a criminal and died beside criminals. He forgave a criminal beside him on the cross and told him on that day he would be with him in paradise. When a woman was caught in adultery and stood condemned, he forgave her, and told her to sin no more. He tells us not to love merely people who are attractive, friendly, and nice to us, but to love even our enemies.

Jesus stands before all the world as the advocate and litigator for the poverty-stricken of society and its fringe members. He tells the world it is wrong in the value it sets on the rich, famous, and successful and in its attachment to them. Jesus advocates and litigates for what the world sees as the bottom of society and tells the world that he will raise the poor up from their poverty to the greatness that he says they deserve. Jesus litigates for a world without division, without dominance, without distinctions of class, wealth, or economic status. Jesus is the ultimate advocate for those whom the world concedes of no value and no importance, for those the country clubs and mansions of the world exclude. He is the litigator for the 98% who are presently powerless before the forces of the world.

Reprinted with permission from Counterpunch. www.*counterpunch.org. April 20, 2011*

Chapter 10
Something about Contraception

The other day, I had a chance to come across and read an OP-ED piece in the May 23, 2012, issue of *The New York Times*. This was an article by Maureen Dowd, a *New York Times* Columnist whom I greatly admire under most circumstances.

Ms. Dowd objects to the position of the Roman Catholic Church concerning contraception. She begins the essay by stating that her parents were devout Catholics. She goes on to say and note her disapproval of Catholic Church leaders' fighting President Obama's attempt to get insurance coverage for contraception for women who work at or go to college at Catholic institutions.

Ms. Dowd argues and insists that the Church's position constitutes some sort of war on women and a way of maintaining women's lower role and caste in the church. She believes the Roman Catholic Church is obsessed with sex in the wrong ways. She says the bishops and Vatican care passionately about putting women in chastity belts, but yet are unconcerned about sexual abuse by priests.

Ms. Dowd is mistaken in her argument, erroneous in her thinking. She believes the Roman Catholic Church to be anti-female and to be conducting some sort of backward prejudicial war by men against women. The issue of free abortion and contraception is concerned with human life. For a Christian, all life, and all human life, all human beings that were ever born or ever existed and whoever will come into being are created by God and in the image of Christ.

Christ and his Church conduct no war against either sex, but place ultimate and eternal value on every person, old, handicapped, about to be born, dying, and about to come into the world to life. I suggest to Ms. Dowd that she look at the Cross, in which we have an image of a God dying and suffering for all mankind. The position of the Catholic Church and of the believing Christian is not concerned with shallow feminist politics, but with who we are as human beings, whoever we may be, and who we are capable of ultimately becoming.

If Ms. Dowd objects to the position of the Catholic Church in this respect, I suggest she consider the value she attaches to herself and her own life. If Ms. Dowd says that abortion and contraception are feminist issues, the Catholic Church, in fact, is not concerned and obsessed with sex, as Ms. Dowd argues, but with the sanctity and worth of all human life, irrespective of race, sex, class, social status, or age. For the Catholic Church, equal value is attached both to the terminally ill about to leave this world and to the infant about to be born. In fact, there is no difference between male and female at all, but the difference in Ms. Dowd's perspective and that of the Catholic Church lies in whom we see our fellow human beings to be in their essential personhood.

I would like to offer another reason for the position of the Roman Catholic Church concerning contraception. Contraception in some sense, if freely distributed and given to all comers, can result in promiscuous sexual conduct. The position of the church is that sexual activity should be confined, on a moral and theological basis, to the marriage bond and when the use of contraception is encouraged, sex as an act of love and connected with the creation of a family becomes nothing more than a means of selfish sexual pleasure. It is the position of the Roman Catholic Church, rightly or wrongly, that sex should occur in the love and nurturing bond of the family and marriage

Contraception and the use of contraceptives strike at the institution of marriage and offers ultimately, as a substitute, free promiscuous sexual activity whose sole object is selfish sexual pleasure.

Chapter 11
A Word on Repentance

Repentance, as a concept in the Christian belief system, posits and means an admission of wrongdoing on the part of the person repenting and general remorse in that admission. Hence, people are told by the church to repent of their sins. Repentance is not excusing and putting aside but an internal admission and remorse. In the West, I think that repentance, since Western societies were Christian in their original structure, was a very significant factor. For example, after the Holocaust, the German government did pay reparations to Jewish families. I make no critical statement, but the Japanese government and citizens have not come to terms or made amends for the awful atrocities that they committed during World War II. The Japanese have never apologized for their brutal treatment of the Chinese and Koreans during the Second World War. The issues of the Korean "comfort women" or the rape of Nan King in China come to mind.

The West repents of its sins. The Turkish government has refused to take responsibility for the Armenian genocide. It is significant that after the Salem Witch trials, the judges who were responsible for these trials publicly repented.

The English slave trade was ended by the Christian, William Wilberforce. It was the New England Churches that led the abolitionist movement for some years. In this sense Western societies grow and evolve. America repents, modifies, and changes. I do not criticize other societies and systems, nor do I know enough to comment on them or how they work, but I know this much. The West comes to terms with its sins, but I surely do not know whether other societies even have the concept of sin and moral wrong and make public admission and modification of that wrong.

I would like to add one more comment here. It is somewhat significant that, under the Christian belief system, Christ will accept a last minute or even last second act of repentance before death. This seems unfair for the righteous and the good person who has led a blameless life. He gets no more reward than the fully wicked person who at the last second of death repents. I can only say that the love of Christ for every human being is that profound. Christ's love is so great for every human being who has ever lived or will live that he will accept that person at the last second of his life. Christ will afford the one who repents the same eternal life and joy that he affords to the person who has lived a completely good and blameless life.

How can we explain this since it is so difficult to understand? I can only say that the value Christ and God set on every human being is so great that he will accept that person as the last second. In short, Christ wants all human beings to be with him and have a relationship with him and will deny no one that chance, even at the last second. We do not know and cannot know whether Hitler or Stalin repented at the last second. If they did, and this repentance were genuine, then they are with Christ along with St. Francis and the disciples.

Chapter 12
A Word about the Catholic Church and the Sisterhood

The other day I read two Op Ed pieces in *The New York Times Sunday Review* of April 29, 2012. One was authored by Maureen Dowd and the other by Nicholas Kristoff. Both of these writers expressed disagreement with the Vatican's and Pope Benedict's taking issue with the Leadership Conference of Women Religious, the main association of American Catholic nuns. I will consider the essay of Ms. Dowd first. In this essay, Ms. Dowd notes the nuns' passion for social advocacy for the poor and points out the recent sexual abuse scandal in connection with Catholic priests. Ms. Dowd takes the position in this essay that the Vatican is somehow persecuting the sisterhood because of their position on social issues as opposed to not adhering to the total dogmatic and Christian position. Ms. Dowd says that the church is going after the women who are the heart and soul of parishes, schools, and hospitals. Ms. Dowd states that the Vatican attacks the nuns' position on contraception for religious hospitals and notes that the Vatican has accused the nuns of pushing radical feminist themes with respect to the ordination of women as priests, of taking a pro-abortion stance, as well as of taking a positive stance with respect to contraception and homosexual relationships. Ms. Dowd states that the nuns have a right to express dissenting views on these issues or at least are entitled to have opinions and engage in dialog. Ms. Dowd is, I think, mistaken in her thinking.

The position taken by the nuns in favor of the ordination of women as priests may be somewhat a popular political position as is the position of approving consenting homosexual relationships. These are popular political themes. What Ms. Dowd fails to grasp is that the Christian church, and the Catholic Church, do not operate on a politically correct basis. The church's position against the ordination of women as priests is not a position suggesting or adhering to some form of discrimination against women. The role of a priest in the Roman Catholic Church is to conduct a sacrifice in the person of Christ. In short, the Roman Catholic priesthood is the successor of the Jewish Political Levitical priesthood. There is a doctrinal and religious issue whether one can have a priestess, for want of a better word, conduct this sacrifice since this would suggest some sort of sexual connection. Thus the Vatican's position opposing the ordination of women in the Catholic priesthood is not a position intended to denigrate the female sex, but to recognize the sacramental and sacerdotal role of the priest, who stands in the stead of Christ and reenacts that sacrifice.

As well, the position of the church opposing abortion and active homosexual relationships again is not an attempt to discriminate against women or homosexuals on some sort of political basis. Better put, the Church is not the world, nor is the Church a House of Representatives. The Church's position against abortion has as its basis the value of all human life, or put more exactly, the recognition that every person has the face of Christ in their being, and every person that has ever lived, or will ever live, were the persons that Christ died for 2000 years ago. The abortion issue does not have to do with women or their political rights, but with the dogmatic position of the church. Obviously there is the same thinking and conclusion with respect to contraception. I am sure that neither Pope Benedict nor the Catholic hierarchy have any ill will or hatred toward homosexuals.

The Church takes the position that active homosexuality is some level of moral wrong, and in that respect, follows the biblical teaching, in both the Hebrew Bible and the New Testament. Homosexuals, as everyone, will always be welcome in the church with open arms, but the church aligns its position with biblical teaching in this respect. Ms. Dowd, therefore, is mistaken in her thinking, as are the Sisters. The move for social justice and concern for the poor is good in every way, but is not the entire dogmatic and moral Christian structure. In short, Ms. Dowd takes a very shallow, albeit popular, political position that misunderstands the nature of church doctrine and why it is and what it is.

Mr. Kristoff reaches the same conclusion. Mr. Kristoff points out the sexual misconduct of Catholic priests and points out the wonderful work of nuns with the poor. Mr. Kristoff is right, but he fails to fully understand that to be a Christian is not to be selective on moral issues or to parrot current political jargon or to ignore moral doctrines that our present world, for one reason or another, is uncomfortable with. Mr. Kristoff and Ms. Dowd promote tolerance as a moral rule and ignore the fact that abortions end millions of lives, as does contraception.

One can disagree with the Church in these teachings, but most certainly its position must be taken into account. In fact, Mr. Kristoff and Ms. Dowd, I suspect, would be uncomfortable with the statement of Jesus in the Gospels that to look at a woman with lust is to commit adultery. The mistake that Ms. Dowd and Mr. Kristoff make is to conclude that the Church's intent in its criticism of the Sisters is an unfair and unjust attack.

The Church's position is to remind the Sisters that they are not running for office and are not entitled to take a popular political position on one end, namely social justice, but decline to take a less popular position, possibly on extremely significant issues involving life and death, and how the Church should function in society, which may not be popular political positions and stances to take.

Chapter 13
Jesus and Women

The Roman Catholic Church has been severely criticized as oppressing women. The main thrust of these attacks has been focused on the Roman Catholic Church's insistence that women be barred from the priesthood and the Church's opposition to abortion. I have explained in my previous book entitled *Essays of a Christian Worldview* that the reason for the Church's position for not permitting women to be Roman Catholic priests is the fact that the priest is conducting or reenacting the sacrifice of Christ in the person of Christ. Thus, it is not a matter that the church is not an equal opportunity employer. Rather, the issue is what a sacrament is and what is occurring at the Eucharist. By the same token, the Church's opposition to abortion, which again is seen as a feminist issue and an attack on a woman's right to choose, is rather based on the idea that people have value, whether they be infirm, old, handicapped, dying, or yet to be born. The church's view is that human life has value for all in light of the sacrificial death of Christ for all mankind. The world measures people by their success, their intelligence, or their position in society. Christ and the church measure people by a different yardstick, not what they have or what they have attained, but whoever they may be at whatever stage of life, whether nascent, potential, or terminal and approaching death.

In fact, Jesus and the church have raised the status of women significantly. A glance at the gospel narratives will reveal this fact. Matthew, chapter 1, verse 18 and following shows that the Son of God is born of a woman and has a human mother. In the 5th chapter of Matthew, verse 27, Jesus states that to look at a woman with lust is to commit adultery. In verse 31, he goes on to state that anyone who divorces his wife except on the grounds of chastity makes her an adulteress. In Matthew, chapter 8, verse 14, Jesus sees Peter's mother-in-law sick with a fever and cures her with a touch of the hand. In Matthew, chapter 9, verse 18, Jesus cures a woman suffering from an illness. In Matthew, chapter 27, verse 55, a number of women are seen following Christ, including Mary and Mary Magdalene. In Matthew 28, verse 1, Mary Magdalene is seen going to the Sepulcher of Christ. In Matthew 13, verse 53, reference is made to Jesus' mother, Mary. Matthew, chapter 26, verse 6 describes a woman who pours ointment on Jesus' head.

In the Gospel of Luke, chapter 7, verses 36–50, again a woman is described as anointing Jesus and kissing his feet. Luke, chapter 8, verse 40, again Jesus cures a young woman. In Luke, chapter 10, verses 38–42, a woman, Martha, and her sister Mary are presented attending to Christ.

In John, chapter 2, the event is presented of Jesus changing water into wine at the marriage in Cana at Galilee. In John, chapter 20, verse 1, Mary Magdalene is presented as coming to the empty tomb. At Jesus' crucifixion at chapter 19 of John, Mary, Mary Magdalene and Jesus' mother are present at the cross. Mary, the mother of Jesus, in the Roman Catholic church is so important that she is referred to as a the Queen of Heaven and can intercede with Christ in prayers directed to her.

This brief review of the gospel material reveals that Jesus, far from degrading women or casting them into a lower societal status, treated them as equals and raised them in status. The Christian faith has always raised the status of women and the ultimate answer to those who state otherwise is to realize that God sent his only begotten son out of eternity to be born of a woman and throughout his earthly ministry was not only constantly in the presence of women, but women were present at the crucifixion and came to the empty tomb at the time of his resurrection.

Chapter 14
Spirituality

The other day, I had a brief conversation with a neighbor of mine in front of my condominium building. I mentioned to her that I was proceeding to a church service, and her response was, "Well, I am very spiritual." I intend no criticism of this person who made this comment, but I do not precisely understand what she meant by this, and I also find that the use of the term has little meaning and misunderstands the nature of religious belief.

What my neighbor meant here, probably, was that like most people, she had some sense of the spiritual or the transcendent. In some sense, that feeling of other worldliness, transcendence, or spirituality is the beginning of religious belief of some sort. It is the beginning point of seeing something beyond ourselves, our own immediate selfish concerns, and the material world and our daily activities in it.

Unfortunately, that is not the Christian belief system. In Christianity, Jesus states that belief and faith in him alone is the only way to have eternal life. Jesus makes many claims on our minds and consciousness. He claims, if not to be God, then to have a connection with God. He tells us that he is the only way and there is no other. He tells us that in the Cross our sins are forgiven, that he rose from the dead, something that no one else has ever done in history, and that by following him and his teachings, we will be remade and regenerated as persons in his image. This is what he means by sonship. He offers us higher ethical standards that are almost impossible to fulfill, such as loving our neighbor as ourselves without the possibility of return from that person; he commands us to give away our goods and live in poverty; he tells us the poor and poor in spirit are blessed; he tells us the meek will inherit the earth and that to look at a woman with lust is to commit adultery: he offers us unconditional love; and he also tells us that in the end there will be a judgment in which we will either gain eternal life with him and have eternal joy and happiness, or suffer eternal death. He tells us that in his sacrifice on the cross, he ended our broken and twisted relationship with God and brought us back into the relationship that we had lost. He tells us that a life devoted to self and material enrichment is a mistake. He tells us the object of life is to serve and not to gain power over others.

In short, I take issue with my neighbor that the Christian religion, or any religion, is to be reduced, if not watered down, to some vague notion of the spiritual or spirituality. That is weak, meaningless thinking and the use of this term to cover weak, meaningless thinking. It allows for religious belief to be shaped and to emerge not from deep and profound thinking but from some sort of feeling good about yourself and others; it implies that by using the terms "spiritual" and "spirituality" you know something and can shape your life and affect and change the lives of others. As a Christian who adheres to the historical Christian faith, as usual I part ways with the use of a term that has no actual meaning and that only serves to darken, obscure, and mislead. At least for me, the creedal, historical Christian faith involves a whole host of thoughts and thinking that represent 2,000 years of theological and philosophical development.

In short, the writings of St. Augustine, the *Summa* of St. Thomas Aquinas, the writings of Calvin, Luther, Bonhoeffer, and John Paul II as well as John Bunyan in his autobiography, *Grace Abounding to the Chief of Sinners*, go far beyond the vagueness and shallowness in confusing profound religious thinking with the coverall term "spirituality."

Chapter 15
Why I Attend Church

In the modern world, church attendance is becoming rare and somewhat misunderstood. I have heard it said by colleagues of mine in the legal profession, both in law school and as lawyers, that they regard going to church and what happens in church as "mumbo-jumbo." They have expressed to me the view that they do not understand why people stand up and sit down during the service, and I have even heard it said that is a kind of primitive magic ceremony.

These people are saying that what occurs in a church service is somewhat nonsensical in light of the scientific advances in the world today. I remember my uncle saying at a family dinner once that he could understand the moral and ethical teachings of Jesus but he felt that everything else that occurs in church is kind of silly. People who maintain this view and say this do not understand the Christian faith and religion and, most of all, do not understand what is occurring at a church service.

I personally am a Lutheran Christian. As Lutherans we believe that at the church service we encounter Christ and relate to him in Word and Sacrament. We are brought initially into relationship with Christ at our Baptism and each time we hear his Word preached and partake in the Communion meal, we grow in relationship.

In sort, non-Christians do not understand that the reason for church-going and the reason every Christian has for being a Christian is to achieve a relationship with Christ on a personal level. Jesus specifically informs us that he offers us eternal life through him. He tells us that he is the mediator and the only way.

At the church service, we meet and encounter Christ, just as we meet and encounter Christ's image in our lives in all persons we may encounter, however long or short those encounters may be.

Church-going is not nonsense, magic, or "mumbo-jumbo." It is the act of faith of every Christian to meet Christ in Sacrament and Word. In the church service, Christ makes himself available, and equally, we in that church service meet him. In the church service and in relating to Christ, we grow as persons in-to the eventual eternal life and joy that he promises to each person and which he wants every human being to have and share with him.

Chapter 16
A Few More Words about Abortion

In a previous book of mine, entitled *Essays on a Christian World View, Political, Philosophical and Others,* I included an essay entitled "Why I Am against Abortion." In that essay, I made the argument that it is an inescapable fact that an abortion either cuts life or ends it in some sense. I concluded by saying that abortion on demand, to end a life in some sense, is to denigrate all persons and conclude they are nothing. To the person who says "unlimited abortion" is okay I say and retort, "What if it were you? Where would you be? And what value do you put on your life?"

In *The New York Times* in its Sunday Review of October 28, 2012, I encountered an OpEd piece by Thomas Friedman entitled "Why I Am Pro Life." Mr. Friedman, perhaps rightly or wrongly, criticizes certain Republican candidates' hard line position opposing abortion, even in the event of rape, and even when the female may be in danger of her life. Mr. Friedman thus criticizes the Republican Senate candidate of Indiana, Richard Murdock, Republican Representative Joe Walsh of Illinois, and Republican Representative Todd Akin of Missouri. Mr. Friedman states that these particular candidates seek to overturn the mainstream consensus in America on this issue. Mr. Friedman states that consensus to be that those who choose not to have an abortion in their own lives by reason of their faith and philosophical beliefs should be respected, but that those women should be respected who want to make a different personal choice of what happens to their bodies and that they should have the legal protection to do so.

Mr. Friedman goes on to argue that the Republicans are incorrectly naming themselves as Pro Life as the Democrats are incorrectly naming themselves as

Pro Choice. He concludes that this is a distortion. Mr. Friedman states that to be against gun control is not to be Pro Life. To shut down the Environmental Protection Agency is not to be ProLife. To oppose social programs such as Head Start, that provides basic education, health and nutrition for the most disadvantaged children, is not to be Pro Life. Mr. Friedman concludes that Pro Life includes those other categories and concerns. Mr. Friedman says that Pro Life is not the proper label to apply to people for whom the sanctity of life begins with conception and ends at birth.

I choose not to repeat the entire argument that Mr. Friedman makes, but essentially he concludes that respect for life should include the things I just mentioned and should have a broader brush. He concludes that the most Pro Life politician in America is Mayor Michael Bloomberg in his ban on smoking in bars to reduce cancer; in his ban on the sale of sugary sods to combat obesity and diabetes; in his requirement to post calorie counts in menus in chain restaurants; in his push to reinstate the expired federal ban on assault weapons; and in his support for early childhood education.

Mr. Friedman, I think, does not understand the issue of abortion. It may be true that there is irony and hypocrisy in the Pro-Life group that opposes abortion and does not support the particular policies Mr. Friedman mentions. In fact, Mr. Friedman does not exactly know who opposes abortion and also supports those policies he mentions. Whether Mr. Friedman sees a consensus on this issue really misses the point, which is the morality of ending a human life in its beginning stages. The issue is a moral issue of stupendous and cataclysmic proportion. Mr. Friedman criticizes the issue's being raised. He assumes a particular consensus at any given time is morally and philosophically acceptable. The fact remains that Mr. Friedman really cannot escape this issue: that if he had been aborted, he would not be writing this column opposing abortion and criticizing the hypocrisy of the political group he may not favor or oppose in this respect.

The error in his thinking is that a woman's personal choice about what happens with her body and insistence that she have the legal protection to do so is a kind of argument but is philosophically incorrect and fallacious. He mistakes the moral issue. The issue is not what a person wants to do with their body, but that a person has been eliminated, if not murdered. That choice is a choice, but the inescapable moral issue is something that Mr. Friedman not does not see, but refuses to acknowledge. A human being who has no choice in the matter has had his life choices removed. If Mr. Friedman wishes to interpret what he finds in those who oppose abortion as backward and hypocritical, I find his argument morally shallow. If he has children, I ask Mr. Friedman that if his children are now born if he would consent to their murder and elimination.

Perhaps Mr. Friedman has to ask himself if his children, whom he now loves and enjoys, had been aborted, what would he make of that? The ultimate question that I ask Mr. Friedman is what he makes of himself at the present tie and what value he sets on the life of his children. Friedman easily argues for the woman's having choice in this respect, and I do not necessarily disagree with him. I do point out to him, however, the disastrous moral consequences of that view. If Mr. Friedman is Pro-Choice, then what does he make of anybody?

I would also like to speak again about an OpEd piece from *The New York Times* on November 4, 2012. There is a column there by Nicholas Kristof. in that column, Mr. Kristof criticizes Mitt Romney. He states that Mr. Romney has taken the position that life begins at conceptions and notes that Mr. Romney states that his policy is to oppose abortion with three exceptions: rape, incest, and cases when the life of the mother is at stake. He notes that Mr. Romney has endorsed a "personhood initiative that treats a fertilized egg as legal person." He notes that Mr. Romney seems to have jumped on the Republican policy bandwagon to tighten abortions.

Mr. Kristof also criticizes Mr. Romney's opposition to contraceptives. Mr. Kristof, in all fairness, says that not just women should be offended by these views, but all of us. What Mr. Kristof regards as backward is in the eye of the beholder. Mr. Kristof says that there was as issue in the last political campaign, that there was some sort of war on women. The fallacy in Mr. Kristof's reasoning and argument is that he evades the essential moral issue. He calls those who oppose abortion "backward." I ask Mr. Kristof that if he had been aborted—and his parent and children—where would they be? The essential moral issue is what moral value should and may be placed on a person. If Mr. Kristof says that my valuation system is backward, then I find his evasion of this issue extremely backward.

Mr. Kristof rightly concludes that the Republican position on this issue is a political issue. I respond that this is not a feminist issue, or a woman's issue, but a human issue. Mr. Kristof concludes and argues that the Pro Life people are anti-woman and anti-woman's rights. That position and argument have little connection with the actual moral issue. Mr. Kristof easily concludes that there is some sort of prejudiced war against women on the part of those who oppose abortion. I counter that he is clouding the issue and the actual issue is what we are to make about any human life, including his own, his children, his parents, and his grandparents. The only war that I see here is a war on the issue: being the life and integrity of any human person at any stage of life.

Chapter 17
The Church: Visible and Invisible

In its beginnings after Jesus' death, the church had something of a struggle to establish itself in the Roman and Greek world. In short, Christians, for their faith and beliefs, were tortured, put to death, and subject to periodic persecution by the authorities. These tortures and executions included crucifixions and putting Christians to death in the gladiatorial arena. As time went on, however, Christianity triumphed and, under the Roman Emperor Constantine, the Christian religion was established as the state religion in the Roman Empire, east and west.

As time went on and the centuries passed, the Church, unfortunately, acted in a somewhat unchristian manner. One cannot account for this, but the fact of the matter is that the church in the Inquisition tortured and killed, usually by burning at the stake, Jews and people perceived as heretics, whether Muslims or Protestants. Indeed, throughout the centuries, both the Protestants and Catholic churches have attacked, killed, persecuted, and tortured one or the other. Joan of Arc was burned at the stake. Protestants in England persecuted Catholics for some time.

One can explain this behavior, which is clearly contrary to the teaching and life of Christ, as a result of the church being societally connected or, better put, a result of the fact that it was more fashionable to be a church member than it is now. So-called Christians made Africans slaves. So-called Christians in England let the Irish peasantry die in the Potato Famine in the 19th century.

I think I would like to offer a better explanation as to why the church, members of the church, and so-called Christians, engaged in obviously great evil and wickedness. The church is composed of weak, fallible, and corrupt human beings. Thus, one must distinguish between the physical, or actual, church on earth which, as I said, consists of sinful human beings, from the invisible church which consists of faithful and believing Christians who not only believe that Christ is the son of God, rose from the dead, and died for their sins, but exhibit this belief in loving, humane, and ethical behavior.

One might even say that many Christians might be found outside of the church walls. Those persons who do not attend church or verbally profess the Christian faith may nevertheless be more actual and authentic Christians than those who make verbal professions within the church institution. Thus, the invisible church which consists of authentic believing Christians, exhibiting Christian behavior, and living the Christian life, is the real and actual church.

The visible church, which not only may and does consist of corrupt and sinful human beings, can also be infected by a corrupt political thinking. One can say only that the invisible church exists; who its members are in some sense we will never know, since only God and Christ, like an x-ray, will examine our souls and hearts and know who we really are. Of course, one cannot exclude and say that authentic Christians are not found in the visible church, but ultimately the church will always consist and ultimately consist of those persons who truly believe in Christ and follow Christ to their death.

When the City of Rome was under siege by so-called barbarians, who now may be found in most of Western Europe, St. Augustine wrote a great book called *The City of God* in which he distinguished between the visible and invisible church. That distinction which he made exists to this day. The church, like any other human institution, whether government, charitable institution, or any other institution human beings may erect, build, and create, will always be corrupted by blackened and sinful human nature which seeks dominance, power, and importance within that institution. The church is not an exception to frail and broken human nature which, in any institution, may ruin the greatness and vision of that institution.

The answer to the critics of the church who point out its defects is that those defects are the defects of everyone of us who all fail as persons. The church does much good and has always done so. Throughout the world, both the Protestants and Catholic churches erect free schools and give free medical care. The church has always done so from its very beginnings and, in the world, seeks out the poorest and most unworthy and seeks to lift them up. The society, however anxious to do so, cannot deny this fact. The criticism that is leveled at the church is a criticism that we must not point the finger at others' doing or others' not doing what they should, or being what they should be as persons, but, we must unfortunately, take a look at ourselves, and whatever defects the church may have are our defects.

At the end of time, the invisible church will be known and those Christians who presented themselves as such for social, faddish, or other reasons will not be counted. I would end this essay with this note: perhaps it is good that it is no longer fashionable to belong to the church, since those who do so now do so at their own risk, and the invisible church may well now be found, in the end, in the visible church as an institution, since in our society today there is no particular political favoritism given to believing Christians. In the end, the invisible church will be and is the true church.

Chapter 18
A Comment on Two Op-ed Pieces

I would like to write about two short essays that appeared in *The New York Times* on February 26, 2012, and March 1, 2013.

"THE WAGES OF CELIBACY"

The February 26th piece was written by Mr. Frank Bruni, and he entitled it "The Wages of Celibacy." In the essay, Mr. Bruni commented on the forced resignation of one of the most senior Roman Catholic clergymen who was accused of unwanted advances toward younger priests. Mr. Bruni says that the celibacy requirement or pledge that the Church requires runs counter to human nature and asks too much. Mr. Bruni says that the requirement for celibacy is foolish and reckless, since it warps the culture of the priesthood and sets an unreasonable standard. He refers to the statement of Cardinal O'Brien that the Church tradition of celibacy is very difficult for the priest to cope with when they feel the need for a companion. Cardinal O'Brien meant by companion, marriage. Mr. Bruni notes that the accusations against Cardinal O'Brien occurred many years ago. Mr. Bruni says that celibacy is a bad idea, has painful consequences, and contributes to the shortage of priests. Mr. Bruni says that celibacy is a trap, falsely promising some men a refuge from the sexual desires that worry them, and results in many gay men going into the priesthood. Mr. Bruni concludes that the promise of celibacy must be related to the Church's sexual abuse crisis.

I take issue with a number of points in Mr. Bruni's little essay. First of all, he presumes that the accusations against Cardinal O'Brien and other priests are true. He makes a series of speculations and outright assumptions about gay men going into the priesthood and that the requirement of celibacy has resulted in the current child abuse crisis. First of all, it is only diocesan clergy who make only a promise of celibacy. Members of religious orders take a vow of celibacy. More to the point, Mr. Bruni is somewhat confused over the reason for the Church's tradition in this respect. Jesus was unmarried and apparently had no other relationships outside of that institution with women or men. St. Paul also was unmarried and recommended celibacy if the person were able to maintain that position in their lives. The reason for the vow or promise of celibacy is that the person undertakes that promise is committing himself wholly and entirely to Christ and His Church without the distraction and responsibility of family and marriage. The Church is asking of its clergy that they follow and imitate Christ in this respect. I would note and think that the Church's monastic orders and communities have their origin in following the example of Christ and his disciples.

Mr. Bruni says the Church asks too much. The Church has asked this and has had no difficulty for a good many hundreds of years of men's entering the priesthood and adhering to this requirement.

The modern world and the media assault us on a daily basis with sexual images and recommendations. Before this media assault, although there may have been individuals who had difficulty with the celibacy requirement, many did not, and many who entered the priesthood fulfilled their lives in the imitation and service of Christ and His Church. When a priest undertakes this requirement, he is following the life of Christ and dedicating himself to Christ, to the Church, and to the love of all humanity. I am not recommending that people not marry, but for the person who undertakes to become a Catholic priest, celibacy focuses his thoughts outward to humanity and Christ and God, and not, in a word, to himself, his wife and family.

I have one other thing to say here and that is that sex, like hunger and thirst, is not to be exaggerated. We may be hungry but we do not eat all day, and we may be thirsty but do not drink all day. We may partake of a glass of water. Like any other human desire, sex must be controlled and channeled into marriage. The media presents the world with a frenzy of continual and continued sexual activity and desire. The Church says otherwise. It says, one, that sex is to be channeled into marriage solely and, two, for those people who want to follow Christ and serve His Church and use their talents solely as a gift of God in the service of others, they are given the opportunity to follow Christ in this respect.

"GIVE UP YOUR PEW"

I would also like to comment on a March 1, 2013, essay in *The New York Times*, entitled "Give Up Your Pew," written by Paul Elie. Mr. Elie says that American Catholics should resign from the Church, like Pope Benedict recently did. He says that America's Catholics are feeling negative about the Church, and that there are things in the Catholic Church that are broken and will not be fixed soon. He observes that it is the season of Lent, where people give up a habit or pleasure. Mr. Elie says again that American Catholics should vacate their pews and explore other religious traditions. He notes that Pope Benedict insulted Muslims and covered up sexual abuse by priests. Mr. Elie says that he will now go to a meeting of Quakers, who have long invited volunteers from his church to serve food to the poor. He says he may go to an Episcopal Church that hosted the Occupy Movement or go to a Zen monastery or attend a Jewish Sabbath Service in Georgetown, Washington, or go to a mosque down the block, or to a Baptist church on his block.

I find Mr. Elie's points extremely weak. Mr. Elie criticizes certain failings of the Church in the form of some comments of Pope Benedict that he takes issue with as well as the purported sexual abuse crisis as reasons to leave the Catholic Church. He gives other reasons. Mr. Elie conveniently fails to notice the massive charitable effort in hospitals, clinics, and education—primary, secondary, and university—that the Church offers all over the world. The Church's dedication to and charitable efforts on behalf of the poor and disenfranchised have long been and are massive. These facts Mr. Elie chooses to ignore and take no note of. Most significantly, if Mr. Elie recommends for himself and others that they leave the Catholic Church and go to some other group, he is reaching the conclusion that the Church's position that in offering the living and resurrected Jesus Christ to the world means nothing to him.

The issue for Mr. Elie is not that he finds the Church inadequate, but that he refuses to understand that the primary message of the Church is the offer of eternal life in Christ. Mr. Elie has every right to choose whatever faith he chooses to embrace, but Mr. Elie must recognized that the choice he has been offered in the Church is to know and fully have a relationship with Jesus Christ, and that is the ultimate choice for all of us. The Church offers in the Sacraments, in the Mass, and in its preaching the message that Jesus Christ is the only way to know ourselves, to fully grow as persons, and to evolve as persons into relationship and sharing with the resurrected Jesus Christ. That is the Church. The Church is Christ, and the issue for me and Mr. Elie is what we may choose to make of the person of Jesus Christ in our lives.

If he finds some other way to be a better person, more fully human in a Quaker meeting or a mosque, those choices may be authentically valid for him. The Church offers Christ to the world, and Mr. Elie can in fact make a perfectly valid choice otherwise, but it is his choice. The choice he is offered by the Church is the person of Christ. We may find in every person and every institution faults and imperfections. Mr. Elie points out the Church's faults and imperfections but fails to grasp that his own imperfections or anyone else's, the imperfections of the government, marriage, the Church are not the issue. He tries to make them the issue but they are not. The issue is what the Church offers to the world, eternal life in Christ, and what he and anyone else in the world intends to make of it.

Chapter 19
Christ and Culture

When I was a student, I had the chance and opportunity to read a very interesting and significant book entitled *Christ and Culture* by H. Richard Niebuhr. The author of this book, a professor at Yale Divinity School, analyzed and considered the interrelationship and interaction between Christ and culture.

I do not pretend to have the depth of knowledge and understanding and scholarship exhibited in this book by Professor Niebuhr. I would like, however, to offer a few thoughts and ideas about the relation and relevance and, if you will, interaction between Christ and culture. The Christian church in its original founding was connected with the Jewish religion and culture. As the Christian religion grew and gained adherence in the ancient world, the Christian religion gradually became more and more prevalent in the Graeco-Roman and became connected with that culture. St. Paul was the original pointing thrust of bringing Jesus Christ and his message and thoughts to Greek culture.

As the Christian Church grew and extended itself, the Christian religion not only became connected with the Graeco -Roman culture, but with the European culture in general. The result was that the church became so connected with the European culture that many poets, artists, and composers became connected with the church and thus with the Christian culture. Many of the major philosophers, theologians, composers, and artists were church-connected, such as St. Thomas Aquinas, Dante, Milton, Bach, Mozart, and many others too numerous to name. Many people came to believe that the European culture was the sole vehicle for understanding the church and its message. Even until very recently writers in the 20th Century such as G.K. Chesterton, T.S. Eliot, Hillaire Belloc, and C.S. Lewis were all active members of the Christian community and church.

Thus it came about that for many Christians the European culture was the Christian culture and, in fact, was the sole vehicle for understanding the Christian message. This is a mistake; it is misleading. One must understand that the Church's function is to present the gospel and bring people into relationship with Christ so that they can evolve and grow, by the term used in the New Testament, "sonship." "Sonship" means that the person not only has a relationship with Christ, but that that relationship is an evolving one of continued growth in Christ. This may be said to be what Jesus means in using the term "being born again."

In sum, the Church's function is to bring souls to Christ. Thus the Church may be found and may function in any culture, whether African, American-Indian, Asian, or wherever the Church may be bringing people to Christ. In sum, the Church has no connection with any particular culture or, in fact, with any form of government. The Church flourished in the later Roman Empire under a monarchy. It continue to function under monarchies in Europe such as the Czar, the French monarchy, and the English monarchy.

The Church has also functioned effectively in democratic countries such as the United States, Canada, Australia, and New Zealand. The Church can be found effectively functioning in countries such as New Guinea or in advanced societies such as are present in the United States and Europe. People who may oppose a non-European message of the gospel make a mistake. They mistake a particular cultural form and artistic expression for the Church's purpose.

This is not to take away from artistic expression, such as the Bach Cantatas or the Gothic cathedral. But to connect European culture with the Christian message is an error. It is true that many fairly educated people may be repelled by the Pentecostal and Baptist churches which are extremely emotional and feeling-oriented in their Christian expression, as opposed to the liturgical, sacramental and more formal Christian expression found in the Roman Catholic and Orthodox churches. Those who are set off by those Evangelical churches mistake the expression of the Church's purpose, which is to bring souls to Christ. That purpose can be found in any group and in any culture, and the face of Christ can be expressed in any number of ways and forms.

In sum, Jesus Christ and the Church have no connection with race, culture, or any particular societal expression. In fact, one may say that Christ and the Church have little connection or concern with cultural expression, however, high-level that expression may be seen as a cultural level and artistic expression. Christ is concerned not with the outward trappings, but with the individual person and soul and with that person's transformation and growth in Christ.

Thus the totally secular person may laugh at the poor and underclass flocking to a Pentecostal or Baptist church. The mistake in their thinking is to understand the Church's purpose, which is not to be what this society thinks it should be whether as more advanced in current thinking or culturally acceptable. Again, the Church does not distinguish in its expression, level of education, or level of culture, but has the purpose and goal of bringing people to a knowledge of Christ and relationship and understanding of him and his offer of eternal life.

Let me add one point. For many years the Protestant church, at least, has been connected with the capitalist system. Max Weber wrote a book about the connection between the Protestant church and the capitalist system. In fact, the capitalist system is quite antithetical to the Church and its message. The capitalist system, in its emphasis on greed. competition, material goods, and the creation of class divisions, in some sense puts people at competitive odds with each other The result is that there is no love in the capitalist system. Love is found in connection, mutual concern, and relationships. The capitalist system, in its functioning and end result by creating a competitive. greed-based, money-oriented—if not hostile—culture where people are pitted against each other, is completely removed from and at odds with the Christian message and ethic. In some sense, not only may the Church function in any culture and economic system but it has successfully done so for for over 2000 years. Perhaps one might account for this by saying that the Church is in any culture, but not of it.

Chapter 20
A Word about Satan

To the modern person the figure of Satan presents itself as a somewhat comical, if not quaint, and ridiculous figure. Satan is seen as a figure with horns and a tail running around and possibly tempting people to do wrongdoing and evil.

To most people, Satan is rather irrelevant to their daily lives and possibly a mythology and fairy tale. Satan, however, is very much a part of the Christian belief system. He first appears leading a rebellion of angels against God, and the purported basis of the rebellion is not acknowledging God's sovereignty over him and not seeing himself as a creature but wanting to be in an equal relationship with God. As a result of this angelic rebellion, Satan is said to have been cast down to hell with his angelic band, but is allowed to roam the earth, tempting people and bringing about evil if he can. God allows Satan to exist until there is a last judgment.

Satan first appears as a snake in the book of Genesis (Genesis 3:1-7). There the serpent says to Eve, "that she will not die, for eating the fruit of the tree which is in the midst of the garden." The serpent misleads Eve, saying that the eating of that tree, she will not die. Satan further appears in First Chronicles 1:1 where Satan is said to have incited David to number Israel. Satan again appears in the Book of Job 1:12 and 2:1-7. Satan is said to be going to and fro upon the earth, walking up and down upon it. Verse 12 in that first chapter says that Satan can exercise power over Job. Mention is made of Job in Zachariah 3: 1-2, where Satan is standing as an accuser of the High Priest.

In the New Testament Book of Matthew, Satan appears in 4:10 where Satan tempts Jesus. Again in Matthew 12:26 mention is made of Satan. In Matthew 16:23 again there is mention of Satan in a conversation with Peter. Again there is mention of Satan in the Gospel of Mark 3:23 and 26, as well as in 4:15 and 8:33. In Luke there is mention of Satan in 4:8, 10:18, 11:18, 13:16, 22:3 and 31. In the Gospel of John, Satan appears in 13:27. He also appears in the Book of Acts 5:3 and 26:18. There is further mention of Satan throughout the New Testament.[1] It is quite apparent that Satan in the dogmatic system is a very real and significant figure.

There are two comments I would make about Satan. First, God allows Satan to wreak havoc and evil in the world until the return of Christ for a final judgment on all men and all creatures, including Satan. What will happen to Satan at that time we do not precisely know. Nor do we know how men and women will be judged; nor on what basis, whether their works alone, their faith in Christ alone, or a combination of both.

What we do know is that whatever may happen to all of us, including Satan, whether we gain entrance into heaven or are cast into hell, God will not destroy us completely and that he will not destroy his creation, Satan, and all men and women. Perhaps that is the awfulness of hell: that for eternity men and women who are cast into hell will be there forever, cut off from the source of being and love, which is God and Christ. One can only imagine that hell is a place of eternal isolation, suffering, and loneliness that will never end for those who are compelled to be there for what they did or did not do in their earthly lives.

The second comment I would make about Satan is to define his fault or failure. The fault of Satan is pride and arrogance. He sees participating in God Go's love that is offered to him, as an insult, as having to have his will bent to a person about him and a higher power. He wants equality, if not superiority, and refuses to recognize God as his creator. This is the essential fault of all men and women, that they wish to be important and that they have such a sense of pride that they do not wish to acknowledge that they are human, that they are creatures, created and not autonomous.

Satan refuses to acknowledge the sovereignty of God and the fact that Satan himself is a created being. Satan wants to run the show. All men and women share that sense of importance, egotism, and refusal to acknowledge the truth that God and Christ are their creator. Satan, in his arrogance, because of his desire to be important, rejects eternal joy and love because of his great pride.

Perhaps John Milton in his epic poem *Paradise Lost* defines the issue more precisely and exactly. Satan is a central character in the poem and Satan says quite explicitly, "Better to reign in hell than serve in heaven." The Christian life is not a life in which the goal is self-importance, but service. Jesus, in the night on which he was betrayed, washed the feet of his disciples, He does the same in our own lives.

NOTES

1. Romans 16:20; 1st Corinthians 5:15. 7:15; 2nd Corinthians 2:11. 11:14. 12:7; 1st Thessalonians 2:18; 2nd Thessalonians 2:9; Titus 1:20. 5:15. Revelation 2:9. 2:13. 2:24. 2:39. 12:9. 12:22 and 12:27.

Chapter 21
Son of God—Son of Man

In the gospels, Jesus refers to himself as the Son of God and the Son of Man. Taking the title of the Son of God is somewhat understandable since Jesus comes to us offering us the doorway to heaven and our way to full relationship with God. There are many references to Jesus referring to himself as the Son of God or being referenced with that term. A few examples from the gospels are sufficient. For example, in Mathew 26:63, the high priest ask Jesus if he is the Christ, the Son of God, and Jesus replies, "You have said so." Again in Matthew 27:40, 43, and 54, Jesus is referenced as the Son of God. Jesus refers to himself as the Son of God and references by others are frequently found using this terminology about Jesus in the four gospels. [1]

It is certainly of no surprise that Jesus would reference himself as the Son of God, communicating to us that he is divine and that he is the way, or rather the portal, to heaven and for relationship with God and himself. It is somewhat puzzling, however, that Jesus should refer to himself as the Son of Man. He refers to himself many times in the gospel or is referred to as the Son of Man. In Luke 21:26, Luke 22:48, and Luke 22:69, Jesus makes very specific reference to himself as the Son of Man. Again in John 5:2, there is a reference to Jesus as the Son of Man. [2]

It is a legitimate inquiry and question why Jesus should use these dual terms about himself. The answer lies in what Jesus wants to tell us about himself and further to communicate his full identification with human nature. By using the term Son of Man about himself, Jesus wishes to tell us he is fully human and not merely some sort of invisible deity. He wishes to communicate to us his full humanity. In some sense, in using the term Son of Man about himself, he wishes us to understand that in his fully human nature he can completely identify with all men and women. By referring to himself as Son of Man, he reaches out to us as human beings and tells us that he is able to understand our difficulties and sufferings. By referring to himself as the Son of Man, Jesus makes possible a relationship with him. He is telling us that he is not some far-removed deity but is fully participating with us or wishes to participate with us in a fulfilling relationship with him and develop in that relation as persons reaching a full level of humanity that would not be possible without him.

It is significant, I think, that Jesus had a full human life and endured the sufferings that all human beings will have to cope with. By using the term Son of Man, Jesus tells us that he will be with us on a human level throughout our lives until the very end when we die. By the use of the term Son of Man, Jesus chooses to present himself in relationship and with understanding and compassion. By the use of the term Son of Man, Jesus tells us that he is with us as a person and not as a far removed God. The use of the terms Son of Man implies participation, relationship, and full understanding. I cannot say what other religions believe about God since I know little of their beliefs and tenets but I think it is significant and important that the Christian God in Christ comes down to us and relates to us. In Jesus' presenting himself as the Son of Man, he is telling us that we will acquire sonship, if you will, and relationship, not as removed but in participation and understanding.

NOTES

1. See Mark 1:1, 3:11, 5:7, and 5:39; Luke 1:35, 22:70, among many other Gospel references.

2. Other examples include John 6:53, 6:62, 13:31; Luke 6:5, 6:22, 7:34, 9:22, 9:56, 9:44, 9:58. See also Matthew 8:20, 11:19, 12:8, 12:32, 12:40, 13:37, 13:41.

Chapter 22
What about God?

Within the past two weeks, specifically on December 24 and December 26, 2012, I had a chance to read two Op-Ed pieces in the *New York Times*. On December 24th, 2012, I chanced to encounter and read an essay by one Rabbi Jonathan Sacks: "The Moral Animal." Again, on December 26, 2012, again on the Op-Ed page of the *New York Times*, I read an essay "Why, God," by Maureen Dowd. I found the reasoning and thoughts in those essays disturbing.

"THE MORAL ANIMAL"

In the one by Jonathan Sacks, entitled "The Moral Animal," Mr. Sacks, the Chief Rabbi of the United Hebrew congregations of the Commonwealth and a Member of the House of Lords, notes that religious belief seems to be in decline; that we live in an age of science; and that there are many prominent new atheists such as Richard Dawkins and the late Christopher Hitchens. Rabbi Sacks asks the question why religion seems to continue to survive in our modern world.

He notes that our societies value altruism and concludes that we are moral animals. Rabbi Sacks concludes that religion is connected with altruism and that religion is a community builder that combines individual into groups through altruism. Rabbi Sacsks states that religion is the best antidote to individualism and the West will never lose its sense of God,

As an orthodox Christian, I find Rabbi Sacks' reasoning weak. He misuses two terms: one "religion" and two "God." I am sure that a Hindu, Moslem,, Christian, or Jewish person would find it quite surprising that their religious beliefs have been downsized and their faith systems have been reduced to some sort of altruism and good works.

Although Christian belief obviously involves good works, I know that it has more substantive core beliefs. For starters, Christians believe that Jesus Christ is the only mediator and route to God and heaven and eternal life. Christians believe that God rose from the dead, died for the sins of all humanity on the cross, and through him we are able to reach eternal life and a relationship with Jesus Christ. Christians believe that Jesus Christ will come again to judge all human beings. Although we do not know when that ill occur, we do know that there will be a time when Jesus Christ will return not only to make a judgment, but to create a new cosmic and world order. Christians believe in a supernatural world called heaven; Christians believe in angels. These beliefs are much more than the sort of vague altruistic behavior that Rabbi Sacks suggests as the reason for the survival of "religion" and belief in God.

Christians believe the things that I stated because Christians believe them to be true and factual. Nobody in any faith has ever believed that being nice has any dogmatic or religious content. The New Testament contains the words of Jesus in the four Gospels. Within four hundred years of the circulation of the manuscripts of the Gospels, virtually the entire Roman Empire became Christian. People do not enter into religious belief and continue to do so, on the vague basis that Rabbi Sacks suggests. People enter into religious beliefs and religious belief systems because they are looking for answers to the ultimate mysteries of life: why do we die; what will happen after we die; why are people found only on earth and nowhere else despite the constant search by physicists and astronomers for other beings; and why are we here. People seek answers to these questions in religious belief systems.

As for myself, I am a Christian because I believe the Christian belief system to be true, and I would ask Rabbi Sacks why, on a daily basis every minute of the day, there are constant Christian conversions all over the world. If religious belief and its content are brought to the point of vague altruism, I part ways with Rabbi Sacks. I am quite sure that every Hindu, every Moslem, and every Jewish person would agree with me that their religious beliefs are much more dear to them than Rabbi Sacks suggests.

"WHY GOD?"

I would also like to discuss the article of Maureen Dowd, "Why God?" Maureen Dowd questions how can you believe in God in view of the recent deaths of 20 children and seven adults murdered in Newtown. Ms. Dowd also notes that she has a 30-year-old memory of the death of a three-year-old. Ms. Dowd remembers visiting a friend before her death and telling her that she believed in the resurrection. Ms. Dowd says that God enters the world through others. Ms. Dowd says that God is experienced in family and community.

Ms. Dowd concludes that God is present in community with others. Let me say that I do not entirely disagree with Ms. Dowd that God is found in the presence of the love of others. What Ms. Dowd fails to understand is that God is found and has presented himself ultimately in the person of Jesus Christ and in relationship to him alone can people know God. This is the core of the Christian belief system. We can only understand our own suffering and the suffering of others, and we can only understand our own death and its apparent finality, when we understand that God, in the form of his only begotten Son came out of eternity, lowered himself to human status, lived as a human being, and was tortured and executed out of love for all humanity.

We can only understand love and the extent of God's love in Christ and his love for all humanity when we can join in the sufferings of Christ, and in that way we can fully understand love in the form of the compassion that Christ offers to all humanity. In sum, when we know Jesus Christ and who he is, the problems that Ms. Dowd describes disappear in the face of his ultimate sacrifice for all mankind.

It is not surprising that people die and suffer when we know the very same people killed and executed the Son of God himself who gave them nothing but love in his early life: joy, healing of sickness and, in the end, through his sacrificial death, offered all men eternal love, eternal joy, and eternal life. It should be no surprise that human beings suffer and die in their early lives when we grasp that this is what they did to God himself in the person of Christ. The mystery of death and suffering is unfolded when we know what humanity has done in that event on the cross two thousand years ago.

Chapter 23
Creation and Fall

The creation story in the first, second, and third chapters of Genesis, which speaks of the creation of man and their fall into sin, is often seen as mere fairy tales or myth. Many persons in the modern secular world, knowing of the scientific advances of society and thinking about them, see these stories as somewhat nonsensical.

The seven day creation story, in the first chapter of Genesis, relates the creation of the heavens and the Earth and the creation of light and darkness (or day and night) on the first day. On the second day, it is said that God said that there should be a firmament in the midst of the waters, separating the waters under the firmament from the waters above the firmament, and God called the firmament heaven. On the third day, God gathered the waters under the heavens into one place and let dry land appear and called the dry land earth and the waters that were gathered together seas. It is further stated that God said that the earth should put forth vegetation: plants yielding seed and fruit trees bearing fruit, each according to its own kind.

On the fourth day, God stated that there should be a light from the firmament of the heavens to separate day from night, and these should be for signs, for seasons, for days and years. It is said that the lights in the firmament of the heavens were to give light upon the earth and that God, too, made two great lights: the greater light to rule the day and the lesser light to rule the night, and He made stars also. All this was done so that the heavens could give light upon the earth to rule over the day and over the night, and separate the light from the darkness. This was the fourth day of creation.

On the fifth day, God said that the waters should bring forth swarms of living creatures and birds to fly above the earth and across the firmament of the

heavens. It is said that God created the sea monsters and every living creature
that lives in the waters and every bird, according to its kind and blessed them
saying, "Be fruitful and multiply, fill the waters of the sea and let birds multiply
in the earth." This was the fifth day.

On the sixth day, God said that the earth should bring forth living creatures:
cattle, creeping things, and beasts, according to their kind. This was the sixth
day and on this day also, God created man in his image. Then God blessed them
and said, "Be fruitful and multiply and have dominion of the fish of the sea, the
birds of the air, and everything that moves upon the earth." God then said, "I
have given you every plant yielding seed and every tree with seed, and you shall
have them for food." God stated that He gives every beast of the earth, every
bird of the air, and everything that creeps on the earth green plants for food. On
the seventh day, God rested and blessed the day. This is the narrative found in
the first chapter of Genesis.[1]

I think upon careful reflection on this narrative in Genesis that I find it quite
intellectually satisfying and in line with science to the extent that I understand it.
The first thing that I find of significant is its sequence. I find it extremely significant that the narrative speaks of the creation of water and dry land, and then the
plants and vegetation occur. This is extremely interesting. The first living creatures that emerge after plants and vegetation are fish in the water and birds. The
theory of evolution, as I faintly understand it, says that life began in the seas and
that after that other life emerged, living beings occurred or made their way on to
dry land. In fact, the Genesis narrative says that the next beings in sequence after
birds and fish are cattle and things that move on the earth. It is quite clear that
this narrative sequence is completely in consonance with many aspects of the
evolution theory that states life emerged from the seas. It is then that man appears at last.

Of course the scientist may argue how can there be days or this sort of sequence when days could not be measured. However, one must understand that
where Genesis narrative parts way with, perhaps moves away from science, is
that God by his thought or spoken word creates. One can question, when there is
no being to measure time and no sun to give us days, how can there be a day or
time. Where Genesis gives its answer here is that God, the creator, is by his
mind and thoughts creating. One cannot know what a day is in the mind and
thoughts of God. One can only say that Genesis tells us that creation occurred in
a distinct sequence of events and that it was only after the creation of the waters
and fish that life emerged on land, and then finally man evolved, came into being, or was created.

Where Genesis parts way from science is that science recounts events and
offers a hypothetical explanation called evolution with no proof other than fossil
remains whereas Genesis says that, yes, life came from the sea, but there was an
act of divine intervention for every sequence that gave forth life. I, for one, cannot quite believe that, even though we see a life coming from the sea to the earth

and various forms of animal life coming forth and finally men and women, this happened by accident or without some sort of cause. All I know is that anything from a pencil to Westminster Abbey or any edifice of any kind, any machine, even a table, has to have been created at some point. Science says that there was a sequence of evolution. Genesis, essentially, says the same but posits a different cause or connection, namely, that the mind and thought of God created this series of events, and the life that Genesis talks about as being created in each sequence and each day.

The earth is a pinprick in the cosmos and life has only been found here. To say that this was an accident begs the question, and I rather believe the Genesis narrative that God created the earth, created all life forms on it—plants, animals, and fish—and that outside of the earth are only the heavens that God describes. Despite far searching by various astronomical devices, no life has been found elsewhere in the cosmos, called in Genesis the heavens. Not only is the Genesis account credible and rational. It bears out the pragmatic findings of science but offers a better and more cogent explanation for these developments and events.

Chapter 2 of Genesis continues the creation event and states that God caused rain to fall upon the earth. Then, God formed man from the dust of the ground and breathed into his nostrils the breath of life. This is the second creation account, it should be noted. Chapter 2 of Genesis then states that God planted a Garden of Eden and put man there, whom he had formed. Out of the ground, God made trees good for food and also in the midst of the garden placed the tree of life and also the tree of the knowledge of good and evil. Chapter 2 then says that God took man and put him the Garden of Eden to till and keep it, but commanded that Adam could feely eat of every tree except the tree of knowledge of good and evil and if Adam did so, God stated that he would die.

The narrative in Chapter 2 then states that out of the ground God formed every beast of the field and every bird of the air and brought them to the man to see what he would call them and that the man gave names to all the beasts, cattle, and birds of the air. Finally at the end of Chapter 2 in Genesis, it states that God caused a deep sleep to fall upon Adam and that he took a rib from Adam and from man made a woman. This is the second Genesis account of creation. It is not part of this essay or article to comment about this other than to say that it differs in many ways from the first Genesis account in Chapter 1.

In Chapter 3 it is said that a serpent advises Eve that although God had commanded that she not eat of the tree in the midst of the garden, the serpent advised Eve that she would not die if she did this. In fact if she did eat of it, her eyes would be opened and she would be like God, knowing good and evil. It is said that the woman saw that the tree was good for food, that it was a delight to her eyes, and that the tree was desired to make one wise. She took the fruit, ate, also gave some to her husband, and he ate. It is said that the eyes of them both were open, and they knew they were naked.

The chapter ends with a short narrative of the Lord God walking in the garden and the man and his wife hiding themselves. When God called to them, "Where are you?" the man responded that he was afraid to speak because he was naked and hid himself. The man explained that the woman gave him the fruit of the tree and he ate. The woman explained to God that the serpent beguiled her and she ate. The chapter ends with God stating that the man has become like a god, knowing good and evil, and God drives them from the garden.

I have a bit to say about this story. The original creation of man is that men were created beings without sin. Not only did they not know good and evil, but had raised themselves above in that sense. It is not a matter that man did not know good and evil but, being in close connection in God, knew only the good. What is significant is that God made a commandment not to eat of the tree of the knowledge of good and evil and told them if they did so it would bring death upon them. The serpent tricks Eve in saying that by eating of the tree they will not die and appeals to that one great failing of human nature: pride and ego. The serpent appeals to that corruption in human nature and says to them that they will be like God.

I don't think that the tree itself was the issue, but the commandment not to eat of it. The mistake that occurred here, and the same mistake as shared by all of us who are human, is that we wish to be gods. Every person wants autonomy, wants total autonomy. Men and women, because of their pride and egotism, reject being creatures created by God and for relationship with Him. The act of eating of the tree was an act indicating the deep-set desire shared by all human nature to be raised above others, if not God. All of us fool ourselves into thinking that we are gods in our lives, that we are totally independent, and that we are totally autonomous, and while we live, we acquire a sense of control and immortality. The mistake that Adam and Eve made was the mistake of us all, thinking that we are equal to anyone including God and including Christ.

The sin of Adam and Eve in the garden was preceded by the sin of Satan, or Lucifer, when he led the angels in rebellion against the rule of God in Heaven. It was Satan's pride and desire for autonomy and disinclination and refusal to serve under God in heaven that led to his condemnation and the fact of his being cast into hell, away from the love, joy, and presence of God. Milton puts it right in his great epic poem *Paradise Lost*. Satan, in *Paradise Lost*, says quite distinctly, "Better to rule in hell than serve in Heaven." Satan and Adam and Eve's mistake is their self-love, their pride, and their essential egotism, their desire for total autonomy, total power, and total reign for their pride, self-love, and gross egotism.

Chapter 24
Jesus the Revolutionary

For many people in the world, Jesus is the ultimate nice guy. He is seen by many solely as the model of the extremely charitable, if not loving, individual. Jesus is seen as caring for all, whether poor or underclass. However, in this essay I would like to consider the question whether Jesus can be seen as a revolutionary. In a previous essay, I presented Jesus as the ultimate litigator for the poor, the underclass, and the outcasts of society. (This essay originally appeared in the magazine *CounterPunch* and forms Chapter 9 of the present book.) I said in that essay that Jesus pointed to a new world system without class, race, or even sex divisions and I presented the view that Jesus was the litigator for the world's poverty stricken and underclass. I noted in that essay that Jesus himself was a carpenter and walked abut with a group of working men, one a tax collector and several fisherman. I said that Jesus was criticized for associating with undesirable people or, better put if you will, sinners. I said that perhaps today Jesus might be seen as a labor organizer or community organizers and certainly showed no particular affinity or admiration for wealth or power and, in fact, said that the poor or poor in spirit were blessed. Jesus approached Jerusalem riding a donkey and was tried and labeled as a criminal. I concluded that Jesus stands before all the world as the advocate and litigator for the poverty stricken of society and its fringe members.

I would like now to talk about whether Jesus can be seen not only as the ultimate advocate for underclass people but even as revolutionary. There is some indication in the four gospels for this point of view. For example, in Matthew 4:18-22 Jesus is presented as inviting several fishermen, including Peter, Andrew, James and John, to be his disciples and follow him. Matthew 5:3 states that the poor and humble are blessed. In Matthew 5:43, Jesus urges us to love our enemies and pray for those who persecute us. In Matthew 9:10, Jesus is seen sitting at a table with tax collectors and sinners. When the Pharisees see this they ask, "Why does your teacher eat with tax collectors and sinners?" Jesus answers that he "came not to call the righteous but sinners."

In Matthew 10:39, Jesus says that he who finds his life will lose it and he who loses it for his sake will find it. In Matthew 12:1, Jesus' disciples are criticized for doing something not lawful to do on the Sabbath. In Matthew 19:21, Jesus advises a young man that if he would be perfect he should go and sell what he possesses and give to the poor; when the man hears this he goes off in sorrow because he has many possessions. In Matthew 19:23, Jesus says it would be hard for a rich man to enter the gates into heaven. In Matthew 21:12, Jesus overturns the tables of the money changers and drives them out of the temple.

In the Gospel of Mark 2:13, Mark notes that when the Pharisees see Jesus eating with sinners and tax collectors and question his doing that, Jesus says that he has come not to call the righteous but sinners. Again in Mark 1:16, Jesus calls not the super smart or super powerful to follow him but fishermen. In Mark 10:21, Jesus again relates to us his advice to the young man to give up his goods to the poor and follow him. Again in Mark 11:25, Jesus advises us that it easier for a camel to go through the eye of a needle than for a rich man to enter the gates of heaven. Also in Mark 10:26-30, when Jesus is asked who can be saved and Peter says to him that the disciples have left everything and have come to Jesus, Jesus says there is no one who has left their house or brothers or sisters or mother or father who will not receive much more, one hundred fold. In Mark 10:43, again Jesus is related as saying you must be a servant or slave to others. Again in Mark 11:15, Jesus is presented as entering the temple and driving out the money changers.

In Luke 6:29, Jesus advises his listeners to offer the other cheek when one cheek is stricken and when someone takes away their cloak not to withhold even their shirt, and additionally to give to everyone who begs from them. In Luke 7:33-39, again Jesus is criticized and is labeled as a glutton, drunkard, and a friend of tax collectors and sinners. In verses 36-50, the story is told of Jesus' being anointed with the hair of an undesirable woman who was labeled as a sinner. In Luke 10:29, in the parable of the Good Samaritan, Jesus tells us that our neighbor is, in that instance, a social outcast, a Samaritan. In Luke 14:7, Jesus advises us that when we are invited to a great banquet we should take the lowest place. In Luke 16:19, there is a story of the rich man and Lazarus. Again in Luke 18:18-23, Jesus gives the advice to the rich young man to sell his goods to the poor and follow him.

What can one conclude from these sayings and narratives in these gospels that I have just summarized? In some sense, these sayings and events present a somewhat radical, if not revolutionary, position with respect to society. Jesus clearly chose to challenge the establishment, or at least the religious establishment. He makes it a point to deny that class or wealth or even outward religious observance is of any particular value. He is criticized, frankly, of associating with people—and making it a point to associate with—the least desirable of people, not merely lower class people (as one might define that group) but even prostitutes, criminals and people on the verge of the criminal class. Jesus wanders about the countryside with a group of mainly working class men, and some women, with no visible source of income. He advises people at times to give up their possessions, to give to the poor, and even says that the poor are superior the wealthy in the eyes of God for some reason we do not know or cannot fathom. Jesus at one point says he seeks to bring not peace but a sword and will divide family members.

In fact there has been a group of persons in the church who have embraced what they have called "Liberation Theology" and have, to some extent, seen Jesus as or in a Marxist context. For example, in Nicaragua some priests in the Catholic Church adopted this position, even advocating some sort of Marxist revolution on behalf of the poor. Clearly these priests sought to address, in this fashion, the gross society abuses in Central America, where—as in South America also—the rich minority have great control over the overwhelmingly poor population of peons, people of African descent, of Indian descent, and of mixed blood.

My conclusion in this: that in these sayings and narratives, Jesus is advising us not only to tend to our affairs but to seek to modify or change society for its present structure of the rich and powerful having dominance and control if they can obtain it. Jesus suggests in these sayings and narratives that the world system is skewed and incorrect in its values and emphases. I do not know whether Jesus is asking us to join in revolutionary action against our present inequitable society and system. To a certain extent, I think he is asking us as individuals to form ourselves in the image he suggests to us, but I might offer the view that he is also asking us to go into the world and improve its present state of confusion and, in many instances, of outright evil.

These sayings and narratives in the gospels can be seen in two lights. In one light Jesus says that by following him in the way that he suggests we can evolve into a better improved humanity, in his image. I thing he is also saying that we should go into the world not to create an outright Marxist revolution but to function in society in the fashion he suggests.

Chapter 25
The Value of the Individual

Many people place a value on others solely on the basis of their wealth and status. For example, men and women who are seeking a marriage partner, I am told, will ask, "What school did you go to?" or "What job do you have?" or even "What car do you drive?" For many people, how the other person dresses and their overall appearance are extremely important. Since marriage is to some extent a "business," or at least economic partnership where mortgages have to be paid and children supported, these are legitimate questions and inquiries. However, this sort of thinking is incorrect and misguided even though very prevalent. People are valued and judged in our society on a money basis. In fact, when people no longer earn money, their value decreases in our system.

The Christian view in this respect is quite different. It is different in two ways. For one, it is the Christian position that God created every person who was ever born or will be born and that God places equal and, in fact, ultimate value on every person regardless of wealth, sex, race, gender or sexual preference. The value that God and Christ place on each of us is incalculable and cannot be measured in human terms. It is perhaps somewhat disturbing, and a source of disagreement to many people, that the church opposes abortion in some instances. This position is based on the value that God accords to all. The act of creation that goes into goes into creating each and every one of us shows God's extreme concern and the importance that he gives to every person, whoever they are and wherever they may be.

He does not distinguish the beautiful from the ugly, the handicapped from the strong, or the old from the young. In creating each of those persons he sets a value—and an equal value—on each of us individually. I would add that in creating people, God exhibits his desire for a relationship with us, again an indication of the value and potential that he sees within us and accords us.

The second basis for Christians to reject the world's economic and greed-based valuation system is that we believe that Jesus Christ died for all, not just a select few. For the Christian, in the crucifixion of Christ the statement is being made to us that the Son of God himself died an agonizing death, not for the people he liked, nor for one group over another group, and not for one race or gender or another, not for the beautiful, but also for the not so beautiful, making no distinction between them. For the Christian community, in the act of Jesus Christ's dying for all who lived and who will ever live, we are told and the message is given to us that God did not stop at death itself to bring people to eternal life with him. One can only imagine the value and importance that God attaches to each of us, to everyone who has ever lived or ever will live, when we realize that he died for each of us. We can only ask the question of ourselves for whom we would be willing to die, when we realize that God died for people who are indifferent to him, perhaps do not like him at all, as well as for those he likes and who like him.

In the creation of human beings and in their redemption by the cross, God is telling us the extent to which he places a value on the individual. He is telling us his view of the love he has for us, a love that did not stop at death. Most important he is informing us of the potential he sees in us to be something greater and more exalted that we can ever imagine. He sees something in each of us that we do not quite understand, but he sees what we can be and are capable of being, which is some sort of magnificent eternal being who will be in relationship, in communication, and in eternal joy with God, and in continued growth to a level that we cannot quite fathom. In creating and redeeming us, God is informing us of the value that he not only presently sees in us as individuals but that he sees in what we can be potentially. Perhaps one can measure the value that God has placed on the individual if in every person we may see and encounter we see the face of the suffering Christ on the cross.

Chapter 26
Angels and Demons

In our society today, at least in the secular West which might be said to include both North America and certainly Western Europe, the idea and concept of angels and demons is, for many people, seen as either mythology or the product of a primitive culture and thinking. In fact, many people might be inclined to laugh at people who have a belief system that includes angels and devils. Yet, for Christians, angels and devils are very real beings and, in fact, are quite frequently mentioned in the Bible, where they are portrayed in various roles and situations. I would like to walk through certain scriptural passages which talk about angels and devils. I am not going to discuss the many references in the Bible to these supernatural beings but will examine a few.

Angels are mentioned frequently in the first book of the Bible, the book of Genesis. For example, in Genesis 16:7-11 an angel finds and speaks to Hagar, the maid of Sarah the wife of Abraham. and converses with her. In Genesis 21:17 an angel calls to Hagar from heaven. In Genesis 22:11 an angel speaks to Abraham when he has been commanded to and is about to sacrifice his son Isaac. For further passages in Genesis referencing the activities in angels see Genesis 22:15, Genesis 24:7, Genesis 24:40, Genesis 31:11, and Genesis 48:16.

Angels are also mentioned in Exodus. In Exodus 3:2 an angel appears to Moses in a flame of fire out of a bush. In Exodus 14:19 an angel goes before the host of Israel between the host of Egypt and the host of Israel. For other passages in Exodus speaking of angel see Exodus 23:20. Exodus 23:23, Exodus 32:34, and Exodus 33:2.

Angels are also mentioned in the Book of Numbers, Book of Judges, the Books of First and Second Samuel, the books of First Kings and Second Kings, books of First Chronicles and Second Chronicles, the books of Isaiah, Daniel, Hosea, and Zechariah and are mentioned several times in the Psalms.[1]

Angels are also frequently featured and mentioned in the New Testament. For example, in the Gospel of Matthew 4:6 when the devil tempts Jesus, there is a mention of angels. Again in Matthew 4:11 after Jesus is tempted by the devil, we are told the angels came and ministered to him. Again, in Matthew 13:39, 41, and 49 there is mention of angels. Similarly in the Gospel of Luke, there are a number of instances in which angels are mentioned. Angels are present when they appear to the shepherds at the birth of Jesus in Luke 2:15. Again, in Luke 4:10 when the devil tempts Jesus, angels are mentioned. In Luke 12:8-9 angels are mentioned as being in the presence of God. Again in the Gospel of John 20:12 two angels are present before the tomb in which Jesus was laid.

In First Corinthians 4:9, angels are spoken of. In First Corinthians 11:10 it is said that a woman ought to have a veil on her head because of the angels. Angels are mentioned again in most of the letters of St. Paul, including the Letter to the Hebrews, and in the letters of Peter and Jude.

I would now like to discuss, based on certain passages in the Bible, what role angels play and what they may do. We do know that angels were created along with the entire universe. In St. Paul's letter to the Colossian church, in chapter 1:15-16, St. Paul states that Jesus created all thing visible and invisible on heaven and on earth. In Psalm 148:2 and 5, the psalm states that God created angels. Angels according to the scriptures have certain tasks assigned to them. For example, in St. Paul's second letter to the Thessalonian church (1:17), it is stated that Jesus will be revealed with his angels. In Acts 12:23 it is stated that when Herod did not give praise to God an angel of the Lord struck him down. Most important, angels are assigned to worship and glorify God. In St. Paul's letter to the Hebrews 1:6, St. Paul writes, "Let all God's angels worship him." See also Revelation 5:11-12. Angels also seem to act as messengers. For example in Acts 27:3-25 an angel visits Paul, bringing him hope and courage as he has to stand trial before Caesar.

These are just some of the things that the Bible seems to say that the angels do and are assigned to do. It is noteworthy that in the story of Sodom and Gomorrah in the book of Genesis, chapter 19, two angels come to Sodom and destroy the city. In the story of the birth Christ in the gospel narrative, angels appear to shepherds. In another example, in Matthew 1:18 an angel appears to Joseph in a dream informing him that the child that Mary is carrying was conceived by the Holy Spirit. Again, in Matthew 2:13 an angel appears to Joseph in a dream telling him to take Mary and his child and flee to Egypt. In Luke 2:8 angels appear to the shepherd and inform them of the birth of Christ. It is quite clear from these examples that angels have fairly prominent roles and duties in the biblical narratives. Angels' roles, it appears, are mainly to praise God in heaven, which is constantly mentioned in the Bible. For example, in Psalm 103:19 and 21 the angels are instructed to praise God.

There appear to be various classes of angels. Mention is made of the sera-phim. For example, in Isaiah 6:1-7 where Isaiah states that one of the seraphs flew to him with a live coal which he had taken with tongs from the altar. Isaiah states that with this coal the angel touched his lips, thereby taking his sin away. The second class of angels is the cherubim. They are mentioned in Genesis 3:24 and Exodus 26:1 and are also mentioned in Psalm 80:1 and Psalm 99:1, as well as in Second Samuel 22:10-11. A third group of angels are the archangels which are mentioned, for example, in I Thessalonians 4:16. The Bible mentions by name the Archangel Michael in Revelation 12:7-9. There is also mention of the Archangel Gabriel in Luke 1:19. The Archangel Gabriel appears also in the Gospel of Luke, where Gabriel says to Zacharias that he stands in the presence of God and was sent to speak with Zacharias that his wife would bear the son, John the Baptist. The angel Gabriel also delivers a message to the Virgin Mary.

There is also the fact that there are a group of fallen angels led by Satan. God gives all beings, including angels, free will, and at some point Satan and his demons chose to rebel against God. This battle between Satan and the holy an-gels is described in Revelation 12:4 and 7-9. In the book of Ezekiel 28:12-19, Ezekiel describes Satan's great beauty, followed by his rebellion. Another indi-cation of Satan's fall can be found in Isaiah 14:13-14.

At a later point in this essay, there will be a discussion of demons and of what they do or are revealed to do in the Bible, but this much can be said. To believe in angels is to believe in one aspect of the true and historical Christian faith and system. One cannot choose to throw out the baby with the bath water or, better put, believe what you will and choose to disbelieve in the reality and existence of angels. The fact of the matter is that there are many appearances of angels in the Bible and accounts of the events in which they engage, and their presence in heaven and on earth at times cannot be argued against. If one choos-es to deny the supernatural realm, then all events and beings described in the Bible can be dismissed. Unfortunately, to do that is to dismiss everything that the Bible says happened including the birth of Christ by a virgin, his resurrection and ascension into heaven, his claim to be divine, and the creation of the world as described in the first chapter of Genesis by the fiat or thought of God.

At one time, I taught a Bible class in a church that I will not name. When I spoke of angels and demons, several parishioners informed me that they thought the reference to angels and demons was a reference to the government or a polit-ical reference. I had the unfortunate responsibility to inform these individuals that angels and demons cannot be translated or transformed into our secular world and cannot be politicized. The Bible operates on a thought plain that we can choose to accept or reject but we should be honest in or rejection of it and if we find the claim of the Bible of the existence of a supernatural realm, supernat-ural evens, and supernatural beings, to be funny or absurd, then we are not un-derstanding the particular claims and thoughts presented in the Bible about the world and us. Angels are as much a part of the system of the world and how we need to understand it. We can simply choose a materialistic vision of the world. This may be the true but that is not the Bible's message whether that message is about angels or the nature or existence of God, and where he resides in another world beyond our comprehension, and where the Bible states we are given the opportunity to dwell in with God in eternal love and joy.[2]

In a previous part of this book I discussed the existence and role of Satan. I will now attempt to explain and discuss demons, which in fact are equally said to exist and do their work in the world. We can choose, as I mentioned, to disbelieve in the existence of angels and, in the same way, we can choose to disbelieve in demons or, to put it another way, fallen angels. The New Testament is quite clear in stating that Satan exists. Jesus is tempted in the wilderness by Satan for 40 days and 40 nights in Matthew 4 and in Luke 4. The devil also, in the Book of Genesis in the guise of the snake, brings about the fall mf man.

What I want to discuss exactly here and attempt to underhand and explain is the existence and role of demons. Jesus is very frequently represented as casting out demons, and there are many references to demons and the casting out of demons in the New Testament. In Mark 1:21-26, Jesus casts out demons from a possessed person in the synagogue. Jesus commands the demons to come out of the man. There are 13 references to Satan or to casting out demons in the Gospel of Mark. In Matthew 4:24, Jesus is said to heal demoniacs. In Matthew 8:16, 28, 31, and 33, Jesus is represented as casting out demons. For example, in verse 16, we are told that people were brought to him who were possessed with demons and he cast out those spirits with a word. In verse 28, Jesus casts out demons from two demoniacs and places them into swine. In verse 33, the herdsmen are said to have fled and to have told everything about what happened to the demoniac. In Matthew 10:32-34, Jesus casts out a demon from a dumb man. In Matthew 10:8, Jesus tells his disciples to go and cast out demons. Demons are mentioned in St. Paul's Letter to the Ephesians 6:10-12. In St. Paul's Letter to the Colossians 2:13-15, there is a reference to demons as powers and authorities.[3] Once again the existence of demons, which is particularly noteworthy and apparent in the New Testament, is very real.

Many people in the modern secular world will counter and say that the events depicted in the New Testament concerning demons and Jesus' casting them out and people's being possessed by demons are a product of a culture without science and medicine. Better put, the secular society will say that these are instances of people afflicted with mental illness. Once again, however, the Bible is quite clear in articulating and stating the existence of Satan, demons, and devils. Those persons who say this is nonsense, mythology, and the product of a primitive culture fail to understand that the Bible tells us different things about the world, and one of the things that the Bible tell us is that there are evil forces in the world and, in particular, that there are specific beings loose in the world called Satan and his followers. The demons referred to in the gospels are very real and do take over people's personalities, causing them to do evil. Those who reject angels and demons, implicitly or explicitly, reject the possibility of a world beyond this world as well as values and thoughts that move beyond the materialistic secularism which presently informs our thinking.

In a sense, to reject the existence of angels and demons is ultimately to reject the existence of the Son of God, the Trinity, and the concept of something beyond this world to which we are headed as persons. To reject these concepts is to reject the potential that we can attain as human beings and the endless possibilities that are offered to us. To confine ourselves to our immediate material world and think of nothing else is to engage in a gross limitation of thinking that leads us nowhere. To believe in the biblical worldview, whether angels, demons, or anything beyond ourselves, is to make an intellectual jump that secularism and materialism do not offer us. To believe in the biblical worldview and concepts is to grow as person. To limit ourselves will ultimately cause us spiritual death and destruction. Faith in the material world alone has no end and no end product and, in some sense, offers us only death as well as both personality and personal destruction. This may be what many people see as true but that truth makes us all nothing.

NOTES

1. For further references to angels and their work in the Hebrew Bible, or Old Testament, see the following references:

"He heard our voice and sent angels . . ."	Numbers 20:16
"The angels of the Lord stood in the . . ."	Numbers 22:22
"The ass saw the angel of the Lord . . ."	Numbers 22:23
"But the angel of the Lord stood . . ."	Numbers 22:24
"The ass saw the angel of the Lord . . ."	Numbers 22:25
"The angel of the Lord went further . . ."	Numbers 22:26
"The ass saw the angel of the Lord . . ."	Numbers 22:27
"He saw the angel of the Lord standing . . ."	Numbers 22:31
"The angel of the Lord said unto him . . ."	Numbers 22:32
". . . said unto the angel of the Lord . . ."	Numbers 22:34
"The angel of the Lord said unto . . ."	Numbers 22:35
"An angel of the Lord came up from . . ."	Judges 2:1
"When the angel of the Lord spake . . ."	Judges 5:23
"And there came an angel of the Lord . . ."	Judges 6:11
"The angel of the Lord appeared unto . . ."	Judges 6:12
"The angel of the Lord said unto him. 'Take . . .'"	Judges 6:20
"Then the angel of the Lord put forth . . ."	Judges 6:21
"Then the angel of the Lord departed . . ."	Judges 6:21
". . . that he was an angel of the Lord . . ."	Judges 6:22
". . . an angel of the Lord face to face . . ."	Judges 6:22
"The angel of the Lord appeared unto. . ."	Judges 13:3
". . . the countenance of an angel of God . . ."	Judges 13:6
"The angel of God came up again unto the . . ."	Judges 13:9
"The angel of the Lord said unto . . ."	Judges 13:13
". . . said unto the angel of the Lord . . ."	Judges 13:15
"The angel of the Lord said unto . . ."	Judges 13:16
". . . not that he was an angel of the Lord . . ."	Judges 13:16
". . . said unto the angel of the Lord . . ."	Judges 13:17
"The angel of the Lord said unto him . . ."	Judges 13:18

"And the angel did wondrously . . ."	Judges 13:19
". . . that the angel of the Lord ascended . . ."	Judges 13:20
". . . but the angel of the Lord did no more . . ."	Judges 13:21
". . . knew that he was an angel of the Lord . . ."	Judges 13:21
". . . good in my sight as an angel of God . . ."	1st Samuel 29:9
". . . for as an angel of God. so is my lord . . ."	2nd Samuel 14:17
". . . to the wisdom of an angel of God . . ."	2nd Samuel 14:20
". . . my lord the king is an angel of the Lord . . ."	2nd Samuel 19:27
"When the angel stretched out his hand. . . ."	2nd Samuel 24:16
". . . said to the angel that destroyed . . ."	2nd Samuel 24:16
"The angel of the Lord was by the . . ."	2nd Samuel 24:16
". . . saw the angel that smote the people . . ."	2nd Samuel 24:17
"An angel spake unto me by the word of . . ."	1st Kings 13:18
"Then an angel touched him and said . . ."	1st Kings 19:5
"The angel of the Lord came again the . . ."	1st Kings 19:7
"But the angel of the Lord said to . . ."	2nd Kings 1:3
"The angel of the Lord said unto . . ."	2nd Kings 1:15
". . . that the angel of the Lord went out . . ."	2nd Kings 19:35
"The angel of the Lord destroying . . ."	1st Chronicles 21:12
"God sent an angel unto Jerusalem to . . ."	1st Chronicles 21:15
". . . said to the angel of the Lord that destroyed. it . . ."	1st Chronicles 21:15
"The angel of the Lord stood by the . . ."	1st Chronicles 21:15
". . . saw the angel of the Lord stand . . ."	1st Chronicles 21:16
"Then the angel of the Lord commanded . . ."	1st Chronicles 21:18
"Ornan turned back and saw the angel . . ."	1st Chronicles 21:20
"And the Lord commanded to the angel . . ."	1st Chronicles 21:27
". . . of the sword of the angel of the Lord . . ."	1st Chronicles 21:30
"And the Lord sent an angel which cut . . ."	2nd Chronicles 32:21
"The angel of the Lord encampeth round . . ."	Psalm 34:7
"Let the angel of the Lord chase them . . ."	Psalm 35:5
"Let the angel of the Lord persecute . . ."	Psalm 35:6
". . . neither say thou before the angel . . ."	Ecclesiastes 5:6
"Then the angel of the Lord went forth . . ."	Isaiah 37:36
"The angel of his presence saved them . . ."	Isaiah 63:9
"And Abed-nego. who hath sent his angel . . ."	Daniel 3:28
"My God hath sent his angel and hath . . ."	Daniel 6:22
"Yea. he had power over the angel . . ."	Hosea 12:4
"The angel that talked with me said . . ."	Zechariah 1:9
"They answered the angel of the Lord . . ."	Zechariah 1:11
"Then the angel of the Lord answered . . ."	Zechariah 1:12
"The Lord answered the angel that . . ."	Zechariah 1:13
". . . so the angel that communed with me . . ."	Zechariah 1:14
"I said unto the angel that talked . . ."	Zechariah 1:19
"The angel that talked with me went . . ."	Zechariah 2:3
"Another angel went out to meet him . . ."	Zechariah 2:3
". . . standing before the angel of the Lord . . ."	Zechariah 3:1
". . . garments and stood before the angel . . ."	Zechariah 3:3
"The angel of the Lord stood by . . ."	Zechariah 3:5
"The angel of the Lord protested unto . . ."	Zechariah 3:6
"The angel that talked with me came . . ."	Zechariah 4:1

"... spake to the angel that talked with ..."   Zechariah 4:4
"Then the angel that talked with me ..."   Zechariah 4:5
"Then the angel that talked with me ..."   Zechariah 5:5
"Then said I to the angel that talked ..."   Zechariah 5:10
"... said unto the angel that talked with ..."   Zechariah 6:4
"The angel answered and said unto me ..."   Zechariah 6:5

2. For further references to angels in the New Testament, see the following passages:

"The angel of the Lord appeared unto ..."   Matthew 1:20
"The angel of the Lord had bidden him ..."   Matthew 1:24
"The angel of the Lord appeareth to ..."   Matthew 2:13
"An angel of the Lord appeareth in a ..."   Matthew 2:19
"... glory of his Father with his angel ..."   Matthew 16:27
"... that in heaven their angel do always ..."   Matthew 18:10
"... but are as the angels of God in heaven ..."   Matthew 22:30
"He shall send his angel with a great ..."   Matthew 24:31
"... not the angel of heaven, but my ..."   Matthew 24:36
"... glory, and all the holy angels with him ..."   Matthew 25:31
"... prepared for the devil and his angels ..."   Matthew 25:41
"... me more than twelve legions of angels ..."   Matthew 26:53
"For the angel of the Lord descended ..."   Matthew 28:2
"The angel answered and said unto the ..."   Matthew 28:5
"The angel ministered unto him ..."   Mark 1:13
"... of his Father with the holy angel ..."   Mark 8:38
"... but are as the angels which are in ..."   Mark 12:25
"And then shall he send his angel ..."   Mark 13:27
"... not the angels which are in heaven ..."   Mark 13:32
"There appeared unto him an angel of ..."   Luke 1:11
"But the angel said unto him, 'Fear not ...'"   Luke 1:13
"And Zacharias said unto the angel ..."   Luke 1:18
"The angel, answering, said unto him, 'I ...'"   Luke 1:19
"In the sixth month the angel Gabriel ..."   Luke 1:26
"The angel came in unto her and said ..."   Luke 1:28
"The angel said unto her, 'Fear not. ...'"   Luke 1:30
"Then said Mary unto the angel ..."   Luke 1:34
"The angel answered and said unto her ..."   Luke 1:35
"And the angel departed from her."   Luke 1:38
"The angel of the Lord came upon them ..."   Luke 2:9
"The angel said unto them, 'Fear not ...'"   Luke 2:10
"... the angel a multitude of the heavenly ..."   Luke 2:13
"... which was so named of the angel ..."   Luke 2:21
"... in his Father's, and of the holy angel ..."   Luke 9:26
"... the angels of God over one sinner that ..."   Luke 15:10
"... was carried by the angel into ..."   Luke 16:22
"... for they are equal unto the angels ..."   Luke 20:36
"There appeared an angel unto him from ..."   Luke 24:22
"They had also seen a vision of an angel ..."   Luke 24:23
"... the angel of God ascending and ..."   John 1:51
"For an angel went down at a certain ..."   John 5:4
"Others said, 'An angel spake to him ...'"   John 12:29

"But the angel of the Lord by night . . ."	Acts 5:19
". . . as it had been the face of an angel . . ."	Acts 6:15
". . . angel of the Lord in a flame of fire. . ."	Acts 7:30
". . . angel which appeared to him in the . . ."	Acts 7:35
". . . in the wilderness with the angel . . ."	Acts 7:38
"The law by the disposition of angels . . ."	Acts 7:53
"The angel of the Lord spake unto . . ."	Acts 8:26
". . . day an angel of God coming into him . . ."	Acts 10:3
"When the angel which spake unto . . ."	Acts 10:7
". . . was warned from God by an holy angel . . ."	Acts 10:22
". . . how he had seen an angel in his house . . ."	Acts 11:3
"The angel of the Lord came upon him. . ."	Acts 12:7
"The angel said unto him. 'Gird thyself . . .'"	Acts 12:8
". . . was true which was done by the angel . . ."	Acts 12:9
"Forthwith the angel departed from him . . ."	Acts 12:10
". . . that the Lord hath sent his angel . . ."	Acts 12:11
"Then said they. 'It is his angel . . .'"	Acts 12:15
"Immediately the angel of the Lord . . ."	Acts 12:23
". . . is no resurrection. neither angel . . ."	Acts 23:8
". . . spirit or an angel hath spoken to him . . ."	Acts 23:9
"By me this night the angel of God . . ."	Acts 27:23
". . . neither death. nor life. nor angels . . ."	Romans 8:38
"Know ye not that we shall judge an angel . . ."	1st Corinthians 6:3
". . . with the tongues of men and of a . . ."	1st Corinthians 13:1
". . . is transformed into an angel of light . . ."	2nd Corinthians 11:14
". . . or an angel from heaven. preach any. . ."	Galatians 1:8
"It was ordained by an angel in the hand . . ."	Galatians 3:19
". . . but received me as an angel of God . . ."	Galatians 4:14
". . . humility and worshipping of an angel . . ."	Colossians 2:18
"From heaven with his mighty angel . . ."	2nd Thessalonians 1:7
". . . in the Spirit. seen of an angel . . ."	1 Timothy 3:16
". . . Lord Jesus Christ and the elect angel. . ."	1 Timothy 5:21
". . . made so much better than the angel . . ."	Hebrews 1:4
". . . of the angel said he at any time . . ."	Hebrews 1:5
". . . Let all the angels of God worship him . . ."	Hebrews 1:6
". . . of the angel he saith . . ."	Hebrews 1:7
". . . who maketh his angel spirits . . ."	Hebrews 1:7
". . . but to which of the angel said he at . . ."	Hebrews 1:13
"The word spoken by angel was steadfast . . ."	Hebrews 2:2
"For unto the angel hath he not put in . . ."	Hebrews 2:5
". . . him a little lower than the angels . . ."	Hebrews 2:7
"The angel for the suffering of death . . ."	Hebrews 2:9
". . . took not on him the nature of an angel . . ."	Hebrews 2:16
". . . and to an innumerable company of angels . . ."	Hebrews 12:22
"Some have entertained angels unawares . . ."	Hebrews 13:2
". . . which things angels desire to look . . ."	1 Peter 1:12
". . . angels and authorities and powers being . . ."	1 Peter 3:22
". . . God spared not the angel that sinned . . ."	2 Peter 2:4
". . . whereas angels. which are greater in . . ."	2 Peter 2:11
"The angels which kept not their first . . ."	Jude 6:32

". . . signified it by his angel unto his . . ."	Revelation 1:1
". . . are the angels of the seven churches . . ."	Revelation 1:20
". . . unto the angel of the church of . . ."	Revelation 2:1
". . . unto the angel of the church of . . ."	Revelation 2:8
". . . to the angel of the church of . . ."	Revelation 2:12
". . . unto the angel of the church of . . ."	Revelation 2:18
". . . unto the angel of the church of . . ."	Revelation 3:1
". . . before my Father, and before his angel . . ."	Revelation 3:5
". . . to the angel of the church of . . ."	Revelation 3:7
". . . unto the angel of the church of the . . ."	Revelation 3:14
"I saw a strong angel proclaiming with . . ."	Revelation 5:2
". . . of many angels round about the throne . . ."	Revelation 5:11
"After these things I saw four angels . . ."	Revelation 7:1
"I saw another angel ascending from . . ."	Revelation 7:2
". . . with a loud voice to the four angels . . ."	Revelation 7:2
"All the angels stood round about the . . ."	Revelation 7:11
"I saw the seven angels which stood . . ."	Revelation 8:2
"And another angel came and stood at the . . ."	Revelation 8:3
"The angel took the censer and filled . . ."	Revelation 8:5
"The seven angels which had the seven . . ."	Revelation 8:6
"The first angel sounded, and there were . . ."	Revelation 8:7
"And the second angel sounded, and as it . . ."	Revelation 8:8
"And the third angel sounded, and there . . ."	Revelation 8:10
"And the fourth angel sounded, and the . . ."	Revelation 8:12
". . . heard an angel flying through the . . ."	Revelation 8:13
". . . of the trumpet of the three angels . . ."	Revelation 8:13
"And the fifth angel sounded, and I saw . . ."	Revelation 9:1
". . . which is the angel of the bottomless . . ."	Revelation 9:11
"And the sixth angel sounded, and I . . ."	Revelation 9:13
". . . saying to the sixth angel which had . . ."	Revelation 9:14
". . . loose the four angels which are bound . . ."	Revelation 9:14
"The four angels were loosed, which . . ."	Revelation 9:15
"I saw another mighty angel come down . . ."	Revelation 10:1
"The angel which I saw stand upon the . . ."	Revelation 10:5
". . . of the voice of the seventh angel . . ."	Revelation 10:7
". . . is open in the hand of the angel . . ."	Revelation 10:8
"And I went unto the angel and said . . ."	Revelation 10:9
"The angel stood, saying, 'Rise and . . .'"	Revelation 11:1
"And the seventh angel sounded . . ."	Revelation 11:15
"His angel fought against the dragon . . ."	Revelation 12:7
". . . and the dragon fought and his angel . . ."	Revelation 12:7
"His angels were cast out with him . . ."	Revelation 12:9
"I saw another angel fly in the midst . . ."	Revelation 14:6
"And there followed another angel . . ."	Revelation 14:8
"The third angel followed them, saying . . ."	Revelation 14:9
". . . in the presence of the holy angel . . ."	Revelation 14:10
"Another angel came out of the temple . . ."	Revelation 14:15
"Another angel came out of the temple . . ."	Revelation 14:17
"Another angel came out from the altar . . ."	Revelation 14:18
"The angel thrust his sickle into . . ."	Revelation 14:19

"... seven angels having the seven last ..."	Revelation 15:1
"The seven angels came out of the ..."	Revelation 15:6
"... of the seven angels were fulfilled ..."	Revelation 15:7
"... the temple saying to the seven angels ..."	Revelation 16:1
"The second angel poured out his vial ..."	Revelation 16:3
"The third angel poured out his vial ..."	Revelation 16:4
"I heard the angel of the waters say ..."	Revelation 16:5
"The fourth angel poured out his vial ..."	Revelation 16:8
"The fifth angel poured out his vial ..."	Revelation 16:10
"The sixth angel poured out his vial ..."	Revelation 16:12
"The seventh angel poured out his vial ..."	Revelation 16:17
"... seven angels which had the seven vials ..."	Revelation 17:1
"The angel said unto me. 'Wherefore ...'"	Revelation 17:7
"Another angel came down from heaven ..."	Revelation 18:1
"A mighty angel took up a stone like a ..."	Revelation 18:21
"I saw an angel standing in the sun ..."	Revelation 19:17
"I saw an angel come down from heaven ..."	Revelation 20:1
"... came unto me one of the seven angels ..."	Revelation 21:9
"... gates. and at the gates twelve angels ..."	Revelation 21:12
"... of a man. that is. of an angel ..."	Revelation 21:17
"... angel to shew unto his servants the ..."	Revelation 22:6
"... angel which shewed me these things ..."	Revelation 22:8
"I Jesus have sent mine angel to ..."	Revelation 22:16

3. For further references to demons and casting out demons see Matthew 12:24; 12:27-28.

"... them that were possessed with demons ..."	Mark 1:32
"... diseases and cast out many demons ..."	Mark 1:34
"... and suffered not the demons to speak ..."	Mark 1:34
"... all Galilee and cast out demons ..."	Mark 1:39
"... heal sicknesses and to cast out demons ..."	Mark 3:15
"... of the demons he casteth out demons ..."	Mark 3:22
"All the demons besought him. saying ..."	Mark 5:12
"... and they cast out many demons and ..."	Mark 6:13
"... saw one casting out demons in thy name ..."	Mark 9:38
"... out of whom he had cast out seven demons ..."	Mark 16:9
"In my name they shall cast out demons ..."	Mark 16:17
"Demons also came out of many. crying ..."	Luke 4:41
"... out of whom went seven demons ..."	Luke 8:2
"... man. which had demons long time ..."	Luke 8:27
"... because many demons were entered into .."	Luke 8:30
"Then went the demons out of the man ..."	Luke 8:33
"... out of whom the demons were departed ..."	Luke 8:35
"... was possessed of the demons. was healed ..."	Luke 8:36
"Now the man out of whom the demons ..."	Luke 8:38
"... power and authority over all demons ..."	Luke 9:1
"... saw one casting out demons in thy name ..."	Luke 9:49
"Even the demons are subject unto us ..."	Luke 10:17
"... said he casteth out demons through ..."	Luke 11:15
"... Beezlebub. the chief of demons ..."	Luke 11:15

"... I cast out demons through Beezlebub ..."					Luke 11:18
"... and if by Beezlebub I cast out demons ..."					Luke 11:19
"... with the finger of God cast out demons ..."					Luke 11:20
"... that fox. Behold, I cast out demons ..."					Luke 13:32
"... sacrifice, they sacrifice to demons ..."					1 Corinthians 10:20
"... ye should have fellowship with demons ..."					1 Corinthians 10:20
"... cup of the Lord, and the cup of demons ..."					1 Corinthians 10:21
"... table, and of the table of demons ..."					1 Corinthians 10:21
"... spirits and doctrines of demons ..."					1 Timothy 4:1
"The demons also believe and tremble ..."					James 2:19
"... that they should not worship demons ..."					Revelation 9:20
"... for they are the spirits of demons ..."					Revelation 16:14
"... and is become the habitation of demons ..."					Revelation 18:2

Chapter 27
Why I Should Be Condemned

At first glance many people would perhaps find this subject and concept somewhat comical or would not understand it. However, after much reflection I have reached this conclusion concerning myself and how I have lived my life. When I was a younger person, in general, I felt extremely well of myself in every way. Particularly, as I was studying in college, law school, and graduate school, I thought of myself, first of all, to be very smart, articulate, well-educated, well-mannered. I also though myself to be a fairly good person or, at least, I perceived myself to be. These conclusions were based on my own essential egotism and self-involvement. I would also add that I found myself rather good-looking and popular.

However, Jesus sets a bar in certain sayings in the gospels that makes me think that I should be condemned. Two particular passages come to mind. One is the Parable of the Last Judgment found in Matthew 25:31-46. In this gospel passage, Jesus tells us that when he returns to earth with all the angels with him, he will sit on his glorious throne and all nations will be gathered before him. He will separate them one from another, as a shepherd separates the sheep from the goats. He will place the sheep at his right hand and the goats at his left. He then tells us that he will say to those at his right hand,

> Come, O Blessed of my Father, inherit the kingdom prepared for you from the foundation of the world. For I was hungry and you gave me food. I was thirsty and you gave me drink. I was a stranger and you welcomed me. I was naked

and you clothed me. I was sick and you visited me. I was in prison and you
came to me."

The righteous will then say to Jesus.

"When did we see you hungry and feed you. or thirsty and give you drink. or
see you a stranger and welcome you. or naked and clothed you. or see you sick
or in prison and visit you?"

The king will then answer, "As you did to the least of these you did it to
me," and he will say to those at his left hand to depart into the eternal fire prepared for the devil and his angels.   Jesus is then said to say.

I was hungry and you gave me no food. I was thirsty and you gave no drink. I
was a stranger and you did not welcome me. I was naked and you did not
clothe me and was sick and in prison. and you did not welcome me."

Jesus then says that these individuals will answer him. "When did we see
you hungry. thirsty. a stranger. naked or sick or in prison and did not minister to
you?"

Jesus will then answer the unrighteous that "as you did not do to the least of
these you did not to me" and concludes with the statement that the unrighteous
who do not do to others in the course of their lives what he tells them to do will
go away into eternal punishment. but the righteous into eternal life.[1]

The second passage which points to me and suggests that I should be condemned is found in the Parable of the Rich Man and Lazarus found in Luke
16:19-31. In this parable. Jesus tells us of a rich man who feasted very well every day, while at his gate lay a poor man named Lazarus. full of sores, who wanted to be fed with what fell from the rich man's table and the dogs came and
licked his sores. Jesus tells us that the poor man died and was carried by the angels to Abraham's bosom and the rich man died and was buried.

While in Hades in torment. the former rich man lifts his eyes and sees Lazarus in the bosom of Abraham. In his suffering, the rich man asks Father Abraham to have mercy on him and send Lazarus to dip the ends of his finger in water and cool the rich man's tongue. Abraham then reminds the rich man that in
his lifetime he received good things and Lazarus received evil thing and that
Lazarus is now comforted while the rich man is in anguish.

Abraham then tells the suffering rich man that a barrier has essentially been
established between those in Hades and those in—for want of a better word—
heaven. The rich man then asks Abraham to send Lazarus, who is dead, to the
house of the rich man's father to warn his five brothers about what may await
them. Abraham says they have Moses and the prophets and they are able to hear
them but even if someone comes from the dead they will not repent. The conclusion of this parable is that if someone will not hear and heed Moses and the
prophets. neither will they be convinced if someone should rise from the dead.[2]

From these statements, or rather parables, I see my gross inadequacy and deficiencies as a person. The message of these parables is clear. It is not enough that we attend to our own affairs, needs, and families. Jesus is quite clear in demanding that we live our lives with a concern, if not love, for those whom we know suffer before us in the course of our lives. Jesus unequivocally states here that there will be a last judgment and that the criteria for that judgment will be how we treat other people. He tells us we must feed the hungry, give drink to those who thirst, welcome the stranger, clothe the naked, and visit the sick and those in prison. Jesus also tells us here that if we do not do these things in the course of our lives, we do the same to him. He is very emphatic and unequivocal in stating that how we treat the least of persons in the course of our lies, we treat him, and that this will be the basis for measuring us as persons and will be the criteria for judgment on us all.

Again in the Parable of the Rich Man and Lazarus, the rich man stood by in fine linen and feasted sumptuously every day while he gave nothing to a poor man, Lazarus, who merely wanted to be fed with what fell from the rich man's table. Jesus tells us that the rich man will be condemned for showing no concern for this very poor person who suffered at his door step while he feasted, and that same person, perhaps because of his very poverty and suffering, will be rewarded. Again, the message here is quite clear that should we live our life with no concern for others and ignore the suffering and pain of our neighbors, who may not in the world's eyes be the best and most desirable, after our lives end the tables will be turned and we will suffer greatly.

Having read and attempting to understand these two parables, I have now reached the very logical and valid conclusion that most of my life has been devoted to myself and that I have done little or nothing for those around me. In fact, I have not visited anyone in prison or sick, have not fed others who needed food, or given clothes to those in need. While I feast with my family during Thanksgiving and Christmas, I do not pay much attention to those who have nothing on those days. It is a fact that I do attend church. However, Jesus makes it quite clear that what matters it is not what I may say about him or whether I profess faith in him but what I do for others and for those whom I may encounter in the course of my life. Perhaps I am no worse or better than anyone else and can only say that it is quite clear at this point in my life that I am a moral failure according to these parables. Perhaps Jesus in these parables sets an impossible bar for all of us. However, he does say this is what we should do with our lives, and if we do not do this, there may be a consequence.

Of course, I am most grateful that at least there is forgiveness by God for my failings. I am fortunate enough to be aware of my failings and I repent of them and hope for forgiveness. I would think I am in the same boat with other human beings trying to survive. However, I now realize that I have spent most of my life thinking of myself and trying to attain things for myself, and I have not given the required consideration and help to the groups to whom Jesus suggests we are obligated. I conclude in weighing the course of my life, my actions, and my thoughts that, yes, I deserve condemnation, but I rest upon the promise of forgiveness and rescue.

NOTES

1. *Matthew 25: 31-46*
When the Son of Man comes in his glory, and all the angels with him, then he will sit on his glorious throne. Before him will be gathered all the nations, and he will separate them, one from another as a shepherd separates the sheep from the goats, and he will place the sheep at his right hand, but the goats at the left.

Then the King will say to those at his right hand, "Come, O blessed of my father, inherit the kingdom prepared for you from the foundation of the world; for I was hungry and you gave me food, I was thirsty, and you gave me drink, I was a stranger and you welcomed me, I was naked and you clothed me, I was sick and you visited me, I was I prison and you came to me."

Then the righteous will answer him, "Lord, when did we see thee hungry and feed thee, or thirsty and give thee drink? And when did we see thee a stranger, and welcome thee, or naked, and clothe thee? And when did we see thee sick, or in prison, and visit thee?"

And the King will answer them, "Truly, I say to you as you did it to one of the least of these my brethren, you did it to me." Then he will say to those at his left hand, "Depart from me, you cursed, into the eternal fire prepared for the devil and his angels; for I was hungry and you gave me no food, I was thirsty and you gave me no drink; I was a stranger and you did not clothe me, sick and in prison and you did not visit me."

Then they also will answer, "Lord, when did we see thee hungry or thirsty or a stranger or naked or sick or in prison, and did not minister to thee?"

Then he will answer to them, "Truly, I say to you, as you did it not to one of the least of these, you did it not to me." And they will go away into eternal punishment but the righteous into eternal life.

2. *Luke 16: 19-31*
There was a rich man who was clothed I purple and fine linen and who feasted sumptuously every day. And at his gate lay a poor man named Lazarus, full of sores, who desired to be fed with what fell from the rich man's table; moreover the dogs came and licked his sores. The poor man died and was carried by angels to Abraham's bosom. The rich man also died and was buried; and in Hades, being in torment, he lifted up his eyes, and saw Abraham far off and Lazarus in his bosom. And he called out, "Father Abraham, have mercy on me and send Lazarus to dip the end of his finger in water and cool m tongue; for I am in anguish in this flame." But Abraham said, "Son, remember that you in your lifetime received your good things and Lazarus in like manner evil things; but now he is comforted here and you are in anguish. And besides all this, between us and you a great chasm has been fixed in order that those who would pass from here to you may not be able and none my cross from there to us."

And he said, "Then I beg you, Father, to send him to m father's house, for I have five brothers, so that he may warn them, lest they also come into this place of torment." But Abraham said, "They have Moses and the prophets; let them hear them." And he said, "No, Father Abraham, but if someone goes to them from the dead, they will repent." He said to him,. "If they do not hear Moses and the prophets, neither will they be convinced if someone should rise from the dead."

Chapter 28
Do Animals Have Souls?

Most Christians, or religious people in general, believe that people have souls. Perhaps what they mean is that human personalities have a kind of permanence and substance that will outlive the grave. Having a soul is generally limited to persons and not to animals. I believe, however, that animals have souls. Not only do I believe that animals have souls, but I think that they will share in the new creation and new world and new cosmos that Christ will bring about upon his return when he will establish his kingdom and the new world order. The reason I believe that animals not only have souls and will in fact share in the new cosmos which Christ will establish upon his return is that I have noted that pets, such as dogs, cats, and even monkeys, can often exhibit great feeling or emotions toward their human masters as well as great loyalty and a close relationship to them..

When the new world order is established, I am convinced that animals, plants, and all sorts of life will be part of this new creation and share in it. I have always observed that in the creation story in Genesis, Adam is given dominion over the fish of the sea and over the birds over the air and over every living thing that lives upon the earth. That chapter also states that God gave to the beasts and birds and to everything that creeps on the earth and everything that has a breath of life every green plant for food. It is clear that in the original creation story in the first chapter of Genesis, Adam has a very direct relationship over the fish, birds, and other animals on the earth, a relationship of dominion. Moreover, in this chapter, plants are also in some sort of relationship as food for the beasts, birds, and animals. It is clear that both vegetation and all living creatures are in relationship to one another and have a mutual dependence and service.

How will I end this little essay? I am of the conviction that animals of all forms have a kind of soul and being, and I think this is true for plants as well. All creation upon the return of Christ, men, beasts birds, and fish and vegetation will be reconstituted and share in the new creation and cosmos as they were originally intended to share.

Chapter 29
The Suffering of Christ:
What Can Be Made of It?

In the four gospels (Matthew, Mark, Luke, and John) the final sufferings of Christ are rather specifically related. For example, in Matthew, chapter 26, it is said that the chief priests and elders of the people gather in the palace of the high priest and take counsel together to arrest Jesus by stealth before executing him. Matthew relates that Judas Iscariot goes to the chief priest and asks what he would be compensated for the delivery of Jesus, and they pay him thirty pieces of silver. Matthew also relates that Pontius Pilate makes a decision not to release Jesus, but to release Barabbas, and then washes his hands of the entire situation. Subsequently in that chapter, it is related that the soldiers strip Jesus, put a scarlet robe upon him, place a crown of thorns upon his head, put a reed in his right hand, and then mock, spit upon him, and take the reed, and strip him of the robe before leading him away to crucifixion. After the crucifixion, Jesus' garments are divided among everyone by casting lots. The events surrounding the crucifixion are stated by Matthew in verses 37-54 of chapter 26.

Mark gives a rendition of these events in chapters 14 and 15. Luke also relates these events in chapters 22 and 23. In the Gospel of John, a similar scene of events is set forth in chapters 18 and 19. These events are widely known to many people and are something of a commonplace, at least in Western society, and where there are conversions in Asia or Arica, these events become more widely known.

Many people may say, "Too bad," and shrug off these events. They might say that a religious troublemaker ran into inevitable difficulties or, at least, had enemies that had moved against him. The wider issue presented by the suffering of Christ is really presented in asking what the sufferings of Christ mean. The more specific issue is what the suffering of any person means to anyone. In many instances, to many people, their lives are busy and they have no concern or time for the difficulties of others. Perhaps they have no real concern at all. There is a small minority of people who may dedicate their lives to alleviating the sufferings of others. They might be connected with the church, but on the other hand, they could be connected with any humanitarian group or organization. These people are a step ahead of the rest of use. But I would like to suggest a deeper meaning to the sufferings of Christ.

The sufferings of Christ point us to the sufferings of others. When we understand and share, intellectually and emotionally, in the suffering Christ we join with him in comprehending, empathizing, and understanding the suffering of all men and individuals. In God's becoming a human being and enduring the great suffering that Christ endured, he joins with us and understands our difficulties and sufferings. Perhaps he knows what each of us, as human beings, is going through, and he grasps our difficulties. He shares our difficulties and deeply moves into them. When we, on the other hand, understand the sufferings of Christ that he endured for all of humanity, he points us to the sufferings of others and brings us to understand and have compassion for the sufferings of others, knowing how he suffered for each one of us to the point of death.

When we understand the sufferings and sacrifice of Christ, we can, to some extent, enter into and fully deal with the suffering that will inevitably come upon us. God became a human being, and suffered for all persons. In that suffering, he tells us who we should be and what we should do. By his example, we are led into the greater and deeper relationship to those who suffer, and we come to understand what their difficulties are and what they are faced with and what we will be faced with.

Chapter 30
The Status of Women

Many people in our present society make the claim that the Church is anti-woman. This statement is largely based on the position of the Roman Catholic Church, and several other churches such as the Orthodox Church, and certain more conservative Protestant denominations that do not ordain women to the priesthood or ministry.

More to the point, many people have lighted upon certain statements or comments about women that Saint Paul makes in his letters. For example, in his first letter to the Corinthian Church, in chapter 7:39 Saint Paul states that a wife is bound to her husband as long as he lives, but if her husband dies, she is free to marry whom she wishes. In that same letter in chapter 11:3-15, Saint Paul states that the head of a woman is her husband. He further states that any woman who prays or prophesies with her head unveiled is dishonoring her head and that if a woman will not veil herself then she should cut off her hair. Saint Paul further states that woman is the glory of man and that women were created for man. He then concludes that that is why a woman ought to have a veil on her head and that in the Lord a woman is not independent of man. Saint Paul further states in the Letter to the Ephesians 5:22 that wives should be subject to their husbands because the husband is the head of the wife and wives should be subject in everything to their husbands. He further states that husbands should love their wives.

In the first letter to the Corinthians 14:34, Saint Paul states that women should keep silence in the churches, since they are not permitted to speak but should be subordinate and that it is shameful for a woman to speak in the church. In the letter to the Colossian church Chapter 3:18. Saint Paul again states that wives should be subject to their husbands.

These statements of Saint Paul must be weight against the entire revelation of the bible about women and their completely equal status. In Genesis 2 we are told that a woman is created as helper for a man. This statement does not mean inequality. It simply means that women in the world have a slightly different role than men. Women create homes and raise families. This does not mean that this activity is inferior or less important than other activities. In the Book of Judges 4:5, tells the story of the judge Deborah who, as a wife, was judging Israel. It is quite clear that this particular story and even should be read, not as relegating a woman in a lesser status, since in fact Deborah had a high society role in Israel.

Let us now look at Jesus' relationships with women in the gospels. In Matthew 2 we are told about the birth of Jesus to Mary. The fact that God himself chose to be born of a woman is a statement of the real status of woman in the eyes of God. The very Son of God was born of a woman and had a mother. In Matthew 5:27. Jesus again raises the status of woman in saying that everyone who looks at a woman lustfully has already committed adultery with her. Again, in verse 31, Jesus states that anyone who divorces his wife, except on the ground of un-chastity, makes her an adulteress and whoever marries a divorced woman commits adultery. Once again, Jesus Christ is significantly raising the status of women in the world. In Matthew 15:21, Jesus heals the daughter of a societal outcast, A Canaanite woman. In Matthew 27:55, Matthew says that many woman follow Jesus from Galilee, among whom were Mary Magdalene and Mary, the mother of James and John. In Chapter 28, Mary Magdalene and Mary went to see the sepulcher after the crucifixion.

In Mark 15:40 we are told that many women looked on Jesus from afar including Mary Magdalene and Mary. When he was in Galilee, they followed him and ministered to him and many other women came up with him to Jerusalem. Again in Mark 16, we are told that Mary Magdalene and Mary were at the tomb of Christ after his crucifixion.

In Luke 1, we are told of the birth of Christ. See also Luke 2:35. In Luke 7:37 we are given the story that a woman of the city, who is a sinner, brought a flask of ointment and, standing at Jesus' feet, wet his feet with her tears, wiped them with the hair of her head and kissed his feet and anointed them with ointment. The Pharisees said, "What sort of person are you? Associating with this sinner?" and Jesus points out to Simon that when he entered his house, he gave him no water for his feet, but this woman has wet his feet with her tears and wiped them with her hair. Jesus says, "You gave me no kiss, but fro the time I came, she has not ceased to kiss my feet. And you did not anoint my head with oil, but she has anointed my feet with ointment." In Luke 10:38-42, we are told that Martha received into her house and that she had sister called Mary who sat at Jesus' feet and listened to his teaching. In Luke 23:36, we are told that the woman who follow Jesus from Galilee stood before him from a distance at the crucifixion.

In John 8 we are told a story of a woman caught in adultery. Jesus prevents her execution. In John 12, again we are told the story of Martha and Mary. Six days before Passover Jesus came to Bethany and that Martha served Jesus and Mary anointed the feet of Jesus with oil and wiped his feet with her hair. See also John 19:25 and John 21.

This essay reveals, I think, that although it is basic and superficial in its examination of the status of women in the church, it is quite clear that both in the Hebrew Bible and the gospels that women have an equal status in society for Jesus. Apparently Jesus had many women friends and women followed him and he had a relationship with them. The passages that I have taken from the gospels clearly reveal that, to put it bluntly, Jesus had no problem with women. Thus, what I have just taken from the gospels and the Hebrew Bible should be weighed against the statement so Saint Paul. Saint Paul was addressing particular situations in the churches he had established. Perhaps his comments about the role of woman may have emanated from his background and culture, had a slightly different view of the role of women in society.

My conclusion is that Jesus not only had women friends but, by his actions, significantly raised the status of woman in his culture.

Chapter 31
Sexuality and Marriage in the
Christian Culture

In our present culture, sex is a hot topic. The reason for this is that sex has become associated with commerce or money. Better put, sex sells! Every magazine we see in a store has a picture of a rather sexually attractive woman. Often
the movies and television programs that are produced seem to feature young,
sexually attractive women and men. Our society in the media rarely features
elderly people. So, one might say that sex is topic and image that is not merely
prevalent in our culture but we are literally inundated with sexual images almost
every day in American society. I have no argument with this myself, but I merely make this observation. There are some people who, barraged with these images and pounded with this sexual message, may come to that that free sexual
promiscuity is the thing to do and the way to live. Obviously, this might be a
mistake, although I make no moral judgment on the person who wises to shape
their lives in this way. Since we live in a free society and unless the action is
illegal, it is permitted. I do add that most people have the wish to and do get
married at some point in their lives. My purpose to discuss here is sex and marriage for a Christian and in the Church.

My view is that sexual attraction, or even lust, is something that we cannot
deal without direction and control. To be hungry and to wish to eat is fine, but
no one would recommend that we eat all the time to the point of gorging ourselves. The same is true of sexual activity or sexual desire. It is not something
that we can simply do with anyone or at any time we want.

For the Christian, God directs lust and sexual desire to a loving union with the opposite sex and to the creation of family. In the say way that we cannot eat anywhere at any time we want, in the Christian understanding God channels lust and desire into a loving relationship and a union which ultimately evolves into the creation of a family.

Elsewhere I have reflected that God uses avarice and greed to create jobs and employment. In spending money and in making money for ourselves, there is a benefit to others in the community through job creation and job maintenance. One may conclude that God uses what can be misused and brings people together in love. Sex unlimited goes nowhere and leads to a kind of destruction. Sex directed in love and in the family union properly channels is God's plan and it is the only possible alternative to societal chaos.

Chapter 32
The Poor and Poverty
in the Bible

There is a general idea abroad that Jesus' concern for, if not identification with, the poor, is confined to the Christian community alone, to the exclusion of other faiths and religious beliefs. It is true that in the New Testament Jesus exhibits a significant concern for the poor. For example, in Luke 4:18 Jesus is said to say in the Synagogue, quoting from the book of Isaiah, "The Spirit of the Lord is upon me, because he has anointed me to preach good news to the poor." Again, in Luke 6:20 Jesus states that the poor are blessed. In Luke 7:22, there is a statement that the poor have good news preached to them. In Luke 14:13, Jesus says, "When you give a feast, invite the poor. You will be blessed because they cannot repay you." In Luke 14:21 in a parable, there is a command to go out quickly to the streets and bring in the poor to the feast. In Luke 18:22, Jesus commands the ruler to sell all of his goods and distribute them to the poor.

In Luke 19:8, it is related that Zaccheaus stood and said to the Lord, "Behold, Lord, the half of my goods, I give to the poor." In Luke 21:23 Jesus says that a poor widow who places in the treasury two copper coins, has put in more than the others. In Matthew 5:3. Jesus states that the poor in spirit are blessed. In chapter 11:5, Jesus says that the poor have the good news preached to them. In Matthew 19:21, again Jesus states to a person who approaches him that if he wishes to be perfect, he should go and sell what he possesses and give to the poor. In Romans 15:26, there is a statement that Macedonia Achaia have been pleased to make some contribution form the poor among the states of Jerusalem. In 2nd Corinthians 9:9, there is a quotation form the Hebrew Bible that the Lord gives to the poor.

It would appear that in the New Testament, and in the gospels particularly, that not only does Jesus exhibit a concern and identification with the poor, but even goes so far as to say that they are superior spiritually, since he refers to the poor in spirit and poor as blessed. One might conclude that this emphasis is solely limited to the Christian church and faith. That conclusion is incorrect since an equal concern for the poor is found in the Hebrew Bible, in particular in the Psalms and Proverbs.

For example in Psalm 10:2, it is said that in arrogance, the wicked hotly pursue the poor. In Psalm 12:5 it is stated that the cause of the poor are despoiled, and because the needy groan the Lord says, "I will now arise." In Psalm 14:6, it is said that the wicked draw the sword and bend their bows to bring down the poor and needy. In Psalm 40:17, it is stated that the Lord takes thought for the poor and needy. In Psalm 41:1, it is said that "Blessed is he who considers he poor and the lord delivers him the day of trouble." See also Psalm 49:2; 68:10, 69:20, 69:33; Psalm 75; Psalm 72:2 and 4; 12–13; Psalm 74:19.

There are similar references in the book of Proverbs exhibiting an eq2ual concern for the poor. In Proverbs 14:21 it is stated that "Happy is he, who is kind to the poor." In Proverbs 14:31 it is stated that "he who mocks the poor insults his maker, but he who is glad at calamity will not go unpunished." In Proverbs 22:9 it is stated that "he who has a bountiful eye will be blessed, for he shares his bread with the poor." See also Proverbs 28:8, 15, and 27; Proverbs 29:7, 13. In Proverbs 31:9, it is said "Open your mouth, judge righteously, and maintain the rights of the poor and needy." In Proverbs 31:20, it is said, "She opens her hands to the poor and reaches out her hand to the needy." See also Proverbs 30:14.

What can be concluded from this examination of the Jewish scriptures which reference concern and consideration, if not obligation for the poor and needy? It is quite clear that concern for the poor is equally found in the Jewish scriptures and is not confined to Christianity. Better put, there is a complete revelation, both in Judaism and Christianity that the poor ought to be assisted and that those who do not choose to do so are in moral error. This is the Judaeo-Christian tradition on this issue.

Perhaps I could put it more exactly, it is the revelation from God to men and women, reminding us and telling us of our moral obligation to the poor and that the poor and needy are to be given upmost love and consideration. I do not know and do not have sufficient knowledge about what other religions may have to say about the poor and of our obligation to the needy. I can only say that the God of Israel and the Son of God command us in this respect. Not only command us, but in the gospels that commands results in the Son of God's telling us that the poor and poor in spirit are blessed and the gospels take a further step beyond the Hebrew Bible in this respect.

Chapter 33
Sonship

In certain sections of the New Testament, there is the discussion or use of the term "sonship." I would like to talk somewhat about those passages. In Saint Paul's letter to the Romans, chapter 8, verse 29 says "for those whom he foreknew, he also predestined to be conformed to the image of his son, in order that he be the first-born among many brother." Saint Paul's Letter to the Galatians states the following:

> I mean that the heir, as long as he is a child, is no better than a slave, though he is the owner of all the estate; but he is under guardians and trustees until the date set by the father. So with us. When we were children, we were slaves to the elemental spirits of the universe. But when the time had fully come, God sent forth his Son, born of a woman, born under the law, to redeem those who were under the law so that we might receive adoption as sons. And because you are sons, God has sent the Spirit of his Son into our hearts, crying, 'Abba! Father!' So through God you are no longer a slave but a son, and if a son then an heir."

Finally, in the Letter to the Hebrews, chapter 12, verse 3, again Saint Paul maintains that God is treating us as sons.

I would like to suggest the meaning of these particular passages. Apparently Saint Paul is directing us to the idea, particularly in chapter 4 of Galatians, that we are being adopted, in some sense, as sons by Jesus. This also seems to be the point in Hebrews, chapter 12. The issue and idea that I wish to examine here is what is meant by "becoming a son."

What I think Saint Paul means here is that we are destined to be eternal beings and as eternal beings, we are adopted into the image and form of Christ. One can say that sonship, or adoption, is being conformed and transformed by Christ into the new sort of man that God wants us to be. It is not that we are mirror images of God or Christ, but that in relationship to him, we become the new man that he has made possible for us.

This is what I think is meant by the reference to being sons and adoption as sons. It means that as we grow in our relationship with Christ, we become more and more like the person that we have the potential to be. What that person will grow to in eternity we can only guess. I can say this much. We will become something wonderful that in this earthly life is beyond our imagination. There will be no barriers, no pain, no death, but only joy, love, and continued intellectual, emotional and spiritual growth as we grow more and more into the likeness and image of Christ.

Chapter 34
A Word on the Patriarchy

Many—to use a word in common parlance—feminists, or women in general, have lately objected to the male terminology found in the Bible. In particular, God is often referred to by the term "Father," and Jesus is referenced with the male term "Son." The first thing that should be said here is that God is a spirit and, as such, has no sex. Therefore, the use of those particular male analogous terms are no more than analogies and we should not come to the conclusion that God is a male with a son. It is somewhat beyond the scope of this essay to attempt to explain the use of these terms in the Bible and in the church. In this little excursus, I will discuss something else more exactly, namely, why Jesus—or so many believe—came to be revealed as a man rather than a woman. I would like, however, initially to suggest an explanation as to the use of these patriarchal terms in both the Hebrew Bible and the New Testament.

First of all, my Hebrew and Greek are, at this point, somewhat amateurish, and therefore I am not n a very strong position to translate the words referencing father and son correctly. I would like to suggest something of an explanation of the use of these patriarchal terms, which many not only object to but seek to change to gender neutral terms in the Bible. I offer the following opinion and analysis.

In the Near East there were many female goddesses and mother goddesses and, not only that, temple prostitution was somewhat common and the reason for this is that people did not understand how food was grown and they thought that, through temple prostitution, they could cause their food to grow. Many of the representations of the female goddesses involved the representation of exaggerated parts of the female anatomy. Thus I suggest, as an approach to the matter , that the patriarchal representation in the Bible is, one might say, God's way of directing us from that that He is some sort of sexual being and that His relationship to us is sexual. Therefore, He uses this terminology to guide us to an understanding that He is not engaged in reproduction. He is not a goddess, and, most of all, He is not some sort of mother goddess as was common in other cultures surrounding the Jewish people at that time. However, I must caution that the use of the male terms is merely an analogy and certainly does not mean that God is a man.

Now I want to talk about something else, namely, another possible explanation as to why God, or so Christians believe, had Jesus come to earth as a man. Again, I am only speculating here, but in the culture at that time, and possibly even today, for a woman to band with a group of women and walk around doing healings and giving ethical discourses and stories to guide people in the form of the parables I do not think was viable in that particular culture. Even today, women who walk about alone, unfortunately, may be seen by certain members of our society as somewhat vulnerable. In addition, a woman at that time, when Jesus came and spoke, probably would not have been accepted in the same way that a man might be in that role. Therefore, I think that the appearance of Jesus as a male was a cultural adaptation and I might be able to say that a woman in the role would not have been accepted or even listened to with same seriousness and attention.

Let me conclude that this little essay with the absolute conviction that God is a spirit and neither male nor female but certainly has the attributes of both sexes. God will render a final judgment, so Christians believe, but also exhibits great compassion and over to all men and women. Of course, it is my personal conviction that love and judgment may be found in either sex, either singly or together, and I think it is a mistake to confine those attributes to either men or women. I think you can find a man as compassionate as a woman, depending on the individual, and a woman able to make critical judgments and decisions with the same ability as a man. Their particular characteristics are not sexual characteristics but personal characteristics.

In short, I think there is a reason for the patriarchal terms in the Bible and the church and I think it is a good reason. I do not think it should be read out of either the Bible or the church since it is there for a very good reason: to inform us about God's nature, which is not sexual. If God were represented as a woman, great confusion could result in human thinking about the nature of God.

Chapter 35
A Final Word on Abortion

For many people, their opposition to abortion stems from a concern for women's rights. I think that this analysis is not quite right. As a Christian, my opposition to abortion on demand stems from the commandment not to kill.

Since we as Christians believe that every person is created, has eternal life, and has an eternal soul and thus has an ultimate relationship with God who not only created him but died for him, my opposition to abortion is grounded in the belief that to kill any human being, particularly an innocent, is prohibited.

In the account of Abel when he is killed by his brother Cain, God declares the wickedness of murder and thus lays a curse upon the murderer. More specifically, in Genesis, Chapter 9:5-6, there is the statement that whoever sheds the blood of a man by man shall his blood be shed, for God made man in his own image. In Exodus, 23:7, there is the statement, "Do not slay the innocent and the righteous." In Matthew 5:21, there is the statement, "You shall not kill." The fifth commandment forbids intentional killing as being gravely sinful.

I have no doubt that human life must be respected in al stages and in every moment. Whether a person is dying, sick, elderly, or beginning life, that life has value. For example, In Jeremiah 1:5, there is the statement, "Before I formed you in the womb, I knew you and before you were born I consecrated you." In Psalm 139:1-5, there is the statement. "My frame was not hidden from you when I was being made in secret, intricately wrought in the depths of the earth." In Job Chapter 10:8-12, there is the clear statement that we are made and created from the very beginning of our conception by God. There are other sections of the Bible that hold the same view.

My opposition to abortion on demand stems from the conclusion that to throw any human being, even one not yet born or just beginning into a garbage can at any stage of life is something that no person can allow. I also note that in the book of Deuteronomy 32:39, there is the statement that God both kills and makes alive. In Job 33:4 there is the statement, "The spirit of God has made me and the breath of the Almighty gives me life." In Job 12:10 there is the statement, "In his hand is the life of every living being and the breath of all mankind." Finally, In Job 1:21, there is the statement, "Naked I came from my mother's womb and naked shall I return; the Lord gave and the Lord has taken away."

In sum, I want to make clear that the abortion issue is not a rights issue, a woman's issue or a man's issue. The dying person, the disabled person, the sick person, the mentally challenged person, and the infant in the womb have the same value. The value that God attaches to all forms of human life cannot be measured.

If I am asked about the death penalty, and personally I do oppose it—it must be distinguished that the death penalty is a punishment by the state against the wrongdoer. This is a different from the life of an innocent whose chance at a full life is cut off.

I offer no solution to whether abortions can be outlawed. I only say that for me the moral issue is as I presented it here. Let me add this from Psalm 139 which for me is proof of God's love for the unborn. Beginning at Psalm 139:13 it states:

> For thou didst form my inward parts.
>> thou didst knit me together in my mother's womb.
> I praise thee. for thou art fearful and wonderful.
>> Wonderful are thy works!
> Thou knowest me right well:
>> my frame was not hidden from thee
> when I was being made in secret.
>> intricately wrought in the depths of the earth.
> Thy eyes beheld my unformed substance:
> in thy book were written every one of them
>> the days that were formed for me.
>> when as yet there was none of them.
> How precious to me are thy thoughts. O God!
>> How vast is the sum of them!
> If I would count them. they are more that the sand.
>> When I awake. I am still with thee."

There can be no doubt that this psalm concludes and ends the issue of unfettered abortion, its morality, and the value that God attaches to all in their stages of life: the dying, the disabled, and the unborn yet to be. Perhaps the most convincing point and argument to present is that every person at whatever stage of life bears the stamp of the divine image.

Chapter 36
Is the Bible To Be Taken Literally?

For many people in the secular society of my world, the Bible is largely irrelevant and is seen rather as a series of fanciful stories. This approach to the Bible does not understand fully what the Bible wants to tell us. The Bible assumes a God in another realm and the existence of the supernatural. The Bible is informing us of God's actions and interventions in human history, from the beginning of the world to the gospel events and the death and resurrection of Christ.

There are a number of ways that people see the Bible and understand it. Some do not see it at all and see it as largely irrelevant. They are fairly happy with their lives, their latest car and their current girlfriend. There is another group of people who may read the Bible as literature. They are a fairly small group. I think they approach the Bible from the wrong angle. The Bible was not meant to be read as literature but as a religious book.

I now come to the issue that I present here. which is whether the Bible is to be taken literally. Quite frankly, I see no other way to understand it. The Bible is the most widely read book in the world and is in fairly constant demand. It has been read and re-read for the past 3000 years. If the Bible were not read and understood in a literal sense. it would have been discarded long ago.

Many people reject the Bible along with other old books and literature as simply not relevant or current. This group may not even see relevance in the Greek tragedies or Jane Austen. Their thought process is fed by some process of absorption from the media and television. The Bible has quite a different approach and the approach has to be understood on its face. The Bible sees people as having fallen from what they should and sees them as failed and in need of restoration. Thus, I read the Bible to find out, literally, what God has to say about humanity, human actions in history, the meaning of life means and the possible outcome of myself as a person. If the Bible is not read as literature, there is no point in reading it at all. It would be the same as reading Shakespeare and not understanding what he is saying literally. In sum, this is true about any kind of book. Not to understand the literal sense of the book is not to understand the book at all.

The Bible, as taken literally, will always and forever supersede any temporary fads or fashions. The Bible tells us that the poor are blessed and advise us to give our material goods. Either one takes this literally or chooses not to. In short, I am not embarrassed about believing the literal truth of the Bible since I am in the company of hundreds of millions of people for the last 3000 years. In short, to read the Bible is to read it as what it says and nothing more. In reading it, we are given the choice of rejecting its content, ignoring it, being indifferent to it, or accepting and applying it. For me, I see no other alternative.

To approach the Bible in an attempt to explain or read away its core or interpret away its contents is taking the wrong road. I realize people may disagree with me about this and I have no difficulty with that. But I have difficulty with any person who says that the literal sense of the Bible has no meanings since long after I am deceased, there will be people all over the world reading the Bible until the end of time.

The issue of the literal understanding of the Bible is found within the Bible itself. In Acts, Chapter 10, Peter specifically states that they were witnesses to all that Jesus did both in the country of the Jews and Jerusalem and that they were witness to his death and resurrection and that the apostles were chosen by God as witnesses who ate and drank with Jesus after his resurrection. These statements of St. Peter in the book of Acts are statements of history and the Apostles were witnesses to the events in the gospels. Again in the Second Letter of Saint Peter, chapter 1, verse 16, Saint Peter states that the apostles did not follow cleverly devised myths but were eyewitnesses of the majesty of Christ. These statements of Saint Peter in the book of Acts and again in his own letter set to rest any doubt as to the historical and literal understanding to be attached to the biblical events.

Chapter 37
A Little Word on the Psalms

From my earliest days when I attended Sunday school, I have been reading the psalms. I recall committing to memory certain psalms, particularly Psalms 1 and 2. The psalms have been called by John Donne, the great Anglican poet and writer, the "manna of the church." The first thing about the psalms is their great beauty. They are essentially what remains of a large body of Hebrew lyric poetry which can also be found in the Psalm of Solomon and in the book of Judges.

The psalms are hymns, essentially. Sometimes they are curses, sometimes they speak of God's judgment on the evil and his reward for the righteous, sometimes they speak of persecution by the psalmist's enemies, and they often exhibit great concern for and exhort us to aid the poor, the needy, and the widows.

The psalms are quite old and how old we do not know precisely. When we read or listen to the psalms, we see the roots of antiquity and, sometimes, see Hebrews dancing and singing these hymns before the Temple. The psalms are old, and many times we do not know their author but they have been ascribed to King David.

I can say this much, one cannot stop reading and rereading the psalms, since they are great lyric poetry. I challenge anyone to read a translation of the psalms in English and a translation of a Greek play or another translated piece of writing and see which they grow tired of more quickly.

It is somewhat beyond the scope of this particular essay to talk about all the psalms (which in a forthcoming book, I intend to do). However, I would like to talk about Psalm 62. I set it here in its entirety.

For God alone my soul waits in silence:
From him comes my salvation.
He only is my rock and my salvation. my fortress: I shall not be greatly moved.
How long will you set upon a man to shutter him. all of you, like a leaning
wall. a tottering fence?
They only plan to thrust him down from his eminence.
They take pleasure in falsehood.
They bless with their mouths but inwardly they curse.
For God alone my soul waits in silence. for my hope is from him.
He only is my rock and my salvation. my fortress: I shall not be taken.
On God rests my deliverance and my honor:
    my mighty rock. my refuge is God.
Trust in him at all times. O people:
Pour out your heart before him: God is a refuge for us.
Men of low esteem are but a breath. men of high estate are a delusion:
In the balance they go up:
They are together lighter than a breath.
Put no confidence in extortion. set no vain hopes on robbery:
If riches increase. set not your heart on them

I have always been stimulated in my thinking by this particular psalm. I
have found a somewhat significant interest in verse 9. That verse states, "Men of
low esteem are but a breath, men of high esteem are a delusion. In the balances
they go up; they are together lighter than a breath." This particular verse has
always struck me with its currency and modernity. The poet says, in his verse,
that there is no difference. in actuality, in class demarcations. Their significance
to the psalmist and poet is meaningless and insignificant. The poet is telling us
here that there is no reality to defining a person by class, since these terms have
no applicability and reality. I find the poet's statements that men of high estate
are a delusion, particularly compelling but he says the same of a person of low
estate having no meaning in being defined by that term, that is, being of low
estate. The poet tells us that taken together, he sees no point in that matter. This
particular poet is making a very advanced statement, namely, that defining a
person by class demarcations is meaningless and in reality means nothing.

In short, when I read this psalm. and one might say any other part of the
Bible, I am in the presence of extremely advanced thinking, which will always
be a challenge to the world's system and the thinking of the soul. To give one
more example, the statement by Jesus that the poor are blessed is an equally
challenging statement and an extreme example of advanced thinking. I challenge
those who say the Bible is irrelevant to read Psalm 62, Verse 9.

Chapter 38
Another Word on Poverty in the Christian Worldview

It is quite clear that Jesus had a particular concern for, affinity and identification with the poor during his lifetime. There are many examples I can refer to. For example, in Matthew 5:3, Jesus makes the statement that the poor in sprit are blessed. Again, in Matthew 22:1–4, Jesus gives a parable called "The Parable of the Marriage Feast." The parable is that the King gives a marriage feast for his son and sends his servants to call those who were invited to the marriage feast. These persons would not come. The King then sends other servants to those who were invited, telling them that the dinner is ready. The persons who were invited make light of the entire situation, and then they seize the servants and kill them. The King is angry and sends his troops to destroy these murderers and burn their city. The king then states to his servants that the wedding is ready but those who were invited are not worthy. He instructs his servants to go into the streets and gather all they find both bad and good.

It is quite clear in this parable that people who will not respond to God or Christ as a person even though they are invited are like the guests who, when they are invited, do not come. It seems to say here that the persons in the streets good or bad will be taken in. Again, there is an emphasis here that God or Christ is no respecter of persons but will take all, even the poorest and most disgraced in the street.

In Luke 6:20, Jesus states that the poor are blessed. Again in Luke 12:15–21, Jesus states that a man's life does not consist in the abundance of his possessions. Later on, in 12:33, Jesus states that when our soul may be required of us, our laying up of treasure for ourselves will do us no good in relation to God.

Again, in Luke 16:19-21, there is the parable of the rich man and Lazarus, in which the rich man pays no attention to the suffering poor man in at his door. When the poor man dies, he is in heaven, whereas the rich man is in hell and torment. We are told that when the rich man requests that Lazarus be sent to cool him with some water, Abraham says that in the rich man's lifetime he received good things. Lazarus received evil things. And now the poor man is in comfort and the rich man in anguish. Again we have a lesson here that when we do not pay attention to the poor, there is the danger that we will be condemned and the poor place above us in heaven and eternal joy.

Again in Mark 2:15 Jesus is criticized for eating with tax collectors and sinners. There is an apparent statement here that Jesus had a positive relationship with the underclass in society. In Mark 10:17-31, there is the story of the young man who asked Jesus what he must do to inherit eternal life and at the end the young man specifically is told that, even though he has obeyed the commandments, he lacks one thing. Specifically, he is told to sell all his possessions, give to the poor, and follow him.

Again we are told here that poverty is a positive quality or attribute in the sense that our riches and possessions may impede our commitment to God and Christ alone. I would add that this particular incident may be interpreted as stating that anything that we may hold onto and put above our relationship to God and Christ, must be given up.

These particular passages that I have chosen are illustrative of Jesus' particular concern for and relationship to the poor and underclass in his society at that time. I would add that Jesus himself worked as a carpenter, or a working man, and that in his three years of ministry there is no indication that he had any material goods or possessions. It is also quite clear that the disciples, in following him, apparently did not bring anything with them, nor is there any indication of their having wealth or possessions. It is quite apparent in reading the four gospels that Jesus mostly associated with the poorer classes in society. In fact he not only attracted their attention by they seem to follow him. On the other hand, the more important individuals, religious leaders or government officials, or the wealthier classes apparently not only in some instances opposed him but apparently did not have much to do with him. The religious leaders at the time were the Pharisees and gave opposition to Jesus.

I would like to end this essay with a general statement that the Christian religion is not an elitist, racial, sexist, or economically based religion. There are times when the rich may have attained control of the Church. However, in general, the Church has taken the position of denial of class, economic, racial and sexual distinctions. Perhaps to understand fully, the connection of the Church and Christ to the poor and poverty, maybe found in St. Paul's letter to the Phillipian Church where he states in 2:5-12 that Jesus himself took on poverty. St. Paul states that Jesus was in the form of God but did not count equality with God, but took the form of a servant. Being in human form, Jesus humbled himself, even to death on the cross. This particular statement of St. Paul explains why the Church has such a great concern for an identification with the poor in society. Jesus himself came down from heaven, and, being God himself, humbled himself to take the limitations of human form, or better put, he took on the limitations of our humanity. There can be no greater act of humility and poverty than what St. Paul defines here. The Church has seen as part of following Christ, not only to exhibit a great concern and identification with the poor, but in some sense, to have the option, ourselves. of giving up our property entirely.

This counsel, and these passages I have just analyzed are what gave rise to the monastic movement where individuals chose to have no possessions and live like Christ and his disciples, unmarried, and obedient.

The Church will never cease in its concern and identification with the poor in the world, since, ultimately. it was God himself who was willing to take on the poverty of our humanity, being, and spirit. It is only when we understand this act of humiliation and poverty that we can grasp why the Church will never cease in its commitment, concern. and love for the poor and all social outcasts.

Chapter 39
Mercy and Judgment

The new pope, Pope Francis, has correctly emphasized the Church's concern with the poor and its emphasis on the mercy and love Christ for all humanity. This is certainly a correct emphasis and articulation since the "good news" of the gospel is the love of Christ for all humanity and his offer of eternal life for those who follow him in there lives. Pope Francis apparently has reached the conclusion that the Church's prior emphasis on legalism and on certain sins was not altogether effective. Perhaps Pope Francis is saying that the Church is not out to condemn sinners but is a place and hospital for sinners, who are all of us.

There is no doubt that there are many passages in the New Testament concerning mercy. In Matthew 5:7 in the Beatitudes, Jesus states that the merciful are "blessed and shall obtain mercy." In Matthew 9:13, Jesus says that he desires mercy and not sacrifice and "came not to call righteous but sinners." In Matthew 9:27, two blind men ask that Jesus have mercy on them. In Matthew 15:22, a woman asks that Jesus have mercy on her daughter whom she states was possessed by a demon. In Matthew 17:15, it is requested of Christ that he exercise mercy on someone's son, who was an epileptic. In Matthew 20:21, two blind men sitting by the roadside ask Jesus for mercy.

In Mark 10:27–28, Jesus is asked for mercy by a blind beggar. In Luke 1:50, mercy again is referred to. In Luke 10:37, at the conclusion of the parable of the Good Samaritan, Jesus is asked, "Who of the three was the neighbor to the robbers?" and Jesus answers, "The one who showed mercy upon him." In Luke 16:24, in the parable of the rich man and Lazarus, the rich man cries out for mercy. In Luke 17:13, ten lepers ask for mercy of Jesus. In Luke 18:38, a blind man begging by the roadside ask for mercy from Jesus.

In these biblical references I have given the reader some basis for the Church's emphasis on mercy and love. However, one must recognize that there is an equal emphasis of mention of Jesus by judgment and one cannot evade this fact. In fact it is an essential part of Church doctrine that there will be a final day of judgment. There are many mentions of judgment in the Gospel. For example, in Matthew 5:21–22, Jesus says that when one insults his brother he should be liable to judgment. He concludes that whoever insults his brother shall be liable to the council and whoever says, "You, fool," shall be liable to hell. In Matthew: 2, Jesus says you should not judge and with the judgment you pronounce you shall be so judged. In Matthew 10:15, Jesus again refers to the day of judgment. In Matthew 11:22 and 24, Jesus again refers to judgment.

In Matthew 12:36, Jesus refers to a final judgment at the end of the ages and specifically states that he will throw evildoers into the furnace of fire where these men will weep and gnash their teeth, while the righteous will shine like the sun.

In Matthew 27:19, again there is a reference to the judgment seat. In Luke 10:14, Jesus again refers to judgment. In Luke 11:31–32, there is a statement that judgment has been given from the Father to the Son. Again in John 5:27 it is stated that the Son of God will exercise judgment. In John 5:30, Jesus states that his judgment is just. In John 12:31, there is a reference again to judgment. In John 7:24, Jesus says that you may judge with right judgment. In John, chapter 16, Jesus again states that he is the judge. In John 16:8, Jesus states that there will be a judgment concerning sin. In John 16:11, Jesus again refers to judgment.

Perhaps the most explicit judgment in the Gospels is found in Matthew 25 beginning with verse 31. Jesus says that there will be a judgment and the judgment will be based on those righteous people who fed the hungry and gave them drink and welcomed them and clothed them, and visit the sick and those in prison. Jesus explicitly states here that those who do not do this will be sent into the eternal fire prepared for the Devil and his angels, stating that when the hungry were not given food, the thirsty not given drink, and the sick not visited and imprisoned, there will be a judgment on that basics.

How do I conclude this little essay about mercy and judgment? There can be no doubt that the Gospel is good news and that it is not a matter of making judgments of any kind but of welcoming and giving to all who come to the Church the mercy and love of Christ. Since all men are sinners and all are imperfect and fall short there can be no alternative but mercy and love. However, we cannot escape the fact that God is a God of justice as well as mercy. Although God mercy and love to us and to all humanity, he does tell us that there will be a judgment. And he tells us the basis of the judgment will be how we lead our lives in relation to others. Perhaps, we must understand the full measure of God's judgment, that the price for sin was the death on the cross of his only begotten Son. The Crucifixion is the measure of God's judgment and the price he chose to pay to redeem humanity and to give them the offer of his unconditional love and eternal life.

In sum, I say this: we cannot escape the fact that God is a God mercy and love as well as a God who abhors sin and is willing to make a judgment. I also say this: we as human beings cannot make any judgment on others. I also say this: if we choose to focus on God's active judgment our concern should not be that nasty neighbor, that unremitting boss, and the sadistic spouse. We must recognize that it is ourselves who will be liable and subject to judgment. If any man or woman cannot accept the doctrine of hell and judgment, then they must understand that hell and judgment are not about Hitler, are not about Stalin, are not about Pol Pot, but are about ourselves.

Chapter 40
A Word on the Fall

For many people in today's world the stories, or better put events, described in the first three chapters of Genesis in the Bible, concerning the creation and fall of man, are seen as myths or fairy tales. After all, what do we have to do with two people in a garden and with a snake that tempts the woman, Eve, to disobey God and eat of a tree that she was told not to. In fact, there are two ways to see the creation and fall events in the Book of Genesis. They can be seen as actual historical events. To understand them as historical or factual, one must grasp and understand that the events described here took place outside our present cosmic world system. Thus we have the option of taking them at the face / factual value.

The way we can understand these events or stories is to see them as allegorical. We can understand them as God's attempting to explain to us how evil came into the world. In presenting these events in the first two chapters of Genesis, he is coming down to our human understanding, in trying to explain to us something that took place outside of human history and outside of our world, in a sense.

I would like to speak for a few minutes about the creation story in Genesis. That story is found in chapters 1–2 of the book of Genesis. In Genesis, chapter 1, God says that he makes man in his image, male and female he created them, and God tells these first parents to be fruitful and multiply and have dominion overall all fish, birds, and living things. It is clearly this creation story envisions a totally different world where there is no violence or hate, and animals, fish, and birds are the servants of our first parents.

There is a second creation story in Genesis, chapter 2 where God forms man out of the dust in the ground, breathes life into him, and places them in the Gar-

den of Eden. In that Garden is a tree of the knowledge of good and evil and a
tree of life, and God commands Adam not to eat of the tree of the knowledge of
good and evil. God then creates a helper for Adam, Eve, taking Eve and creating
her from one of the ribs of Adam. These are the two creations stories in Genesis
chapters 1 and 2.

Now I would like to talk about Genesis, chapter 3, the fall story. In chapter
3, the serpent says to Eve, "You shall not eat of any tree in the garden," and the
woman replies that God had commanded her not to eat from one tree since if she
did so she would die. The serpent says to the woman, "You will not die," that
when she ate it her eyes would be opened and the two would be like God: knowing good and evil. When Eve saw the tree was good for food, that it was a delight to the eyes, and that it was desired to make one wise, she ate of it and gave
the same to her husband. To my sense and thought, the Fall story is a deeply
profound story and one which we must reflect on and seek to understand fully.

The mistake that Eve made was pride. She was told that she would be "like
God." Thus Eve gave into the failing of every person who has ever lived, namely pride. Eve gave into the temptation and reached the emotional and intellectual
conclusion that she was above herself, beyond herself, and equal to God, and not
a created creature. None of us likes to be told we are subject to anyone else and
that we have to do what we are told or commanded. A child will resist obedience
to his or her parents, even though what they wish the child to obey is for their
own good. Pride is the fallacy and mistake to think we are totally independent
and autonomous. Pride is the mistake that our thinking is the right thinking and
good thinking. Our pride always fools us into thinking we are great and greater
than others and better than others.

Eve made this mistake in thinking she could be a god, and it brought about
the entire fall of humanity. None of us wishes to concede our limitation; none of
us wishes to concede our failing; none of us wishes to be sufficiently honest
with ourselves to say we are not equal with God, nor in many senses are we
equal to each other. I will never compose a symphony, write an epic poem, or
play professional baseball. The serpent fooled Eve and lured her into thinking
that she could be something that she could never be and would never be. Pride is
foolishness and stupidity. The pride of Eve resulted in such a destructive fall that
it brought our present world its evil and destructive impulses, to its present situation. This story is true. All of us have shared this fall. All of us are fooled about
ourselves.

The events described in Genesis, chapter 3, I believe happened since I know
that all of us shared in this fall and in this act of pride. All of us are not what we
should be as persons and probably cannot be what we should be as persons because of what happened to Eve and to our first parents. This fall brought about a
twisted, mixed up, and confused world, not the world envisioned b God, a world
where love is shared. Instead we live in a world of constant turmoil and hostility
which ends for all of us in death.

The fall story in Genesis is the truth because we cannot escape who we really are. Its message is our great failing and pride and egotism. The English poet,

John Milton, correctly analyzed the person of Satan in Book Two of Paradise Lost. In Book Two of this epic poem, we have the picture of Satan in his overweening and incredible pride where he states he would rather rule in Hell than serve in Heaven. Satan's pride and rebellion against God led to his destruction. That same pride, he wishes to share with him in Hell. The great sin of Satan, as depicted in *Paradise Lost*, was his arrogance and overwhelming pride. His great desire is to bring the fall of humanity into his thinking and dominion.

Satan was cast out of Heaven because he did not wish to obey and preferred to rule in torment rather than have eternal joy in Heave with God and his angels. He wants us to make the same mistake and constantly presses at our egotism, arrogance, and pride, seeking to bring us down and ultimately bring about our destruction.

Chapter 41
Jesus and Children

One of the most well-known passages in the Gospels is where Jesus invites children to approach him. The incident may be found in the gospel of Mark, chapter 10, verses 13—16. The narrative is that children were brought to him for Jesus to touch and the disciples rebuked the children. Jesus' response was to allow the children to come to him stating that to them belongs the kingdom of God. The narrative ends with a statement that whoever does not receive the kingdom of God like a child shall not enter it and at this point Jesus it is seen as taking the children into his arms, blessing them, and laying his hand upon them. This incident is also found in the gospel of Luke 18:15—17.

This is a somewhat puzzling incident that is difficult for us to truly grasp and understand. The world values strength power, wealth, sophistication, and for lack of a better word, being smart. The world often values people on how they look and dress. Thus when Jesus says, "We are to be like children to enter the Kingdom of God," this is somewhat difficult to grasp. Children are generally seen as innocent, trusting, and obedient. They certainly are not equal in intellect and experience to an adult. Furthermore, no child has ever written a great symphony, written a great book or saved someone's life with surgery, or has had, in general, some form of success. In fact, in the present world, there seems to be great value in celebrities regardless of what kind of person they are on a moral or ethical level. There are all kinds of celebrities perhaps including some morally worthwhile people. However, the great criterion of being a celebrity is having a great deal of money and having our picture and image featured in the media. The society hardly holds infants. ad the benchmark, as Jesus does.

I offer the following analysis and explanation. Children offer to most adults, at least to a certain age, unconditional love. Perhaps Jesus means here that the criteria to enter what he terms "the kingdom of heaven" are humility, unconditional love, and obedience to Christ and God. God does not necessarily want very smart people. In fact it is quite clear that this is an irrelevant quality. It is noteworthy that Jesus chose working men and fishermen to be his first disciples. Perhaps the best way to put it is that only as a child, when our mind is not clouded with lies and falsehoods, can we truly have the sort of relationship to God as he wishes. It is only in the love of a child, the trust of a child, the obedience of a child, and the honesty of a child, that we can approach the Holy God.

Perhaps this particular narrative can be understood only as telling us that the values that the world accords to people and puts upon them are not the true values of an innocent child who is capable of great love, trust, relationship, and, most of all, humility. It is only a child who can understand his true nature to God which involves the qualities as stated above. Perhaps it is possible when we look back at the creation of our parents to recognize that they initially had the innocence and qualities of children. They fell from that innocence and, in that fall, brought evil into the at world with the result of death, destruction, and a humanity that leaves much to be desired, as compared to the childlike innocence of our first parents.

Section Two

Essays on Politics, Culture, and Philosophy and Politics

Section Two – Essays on Politics,
Culture, and Philosophy

Introduction

I have already discussed, in the preface, some of these essays, but I would like to point out others that may be of interest and stimulation. For example, I offer an analysis of the nature of femininity or what truly constitutes the female nature and I reach the conclusion that the main female characteristics are nurturing and sacrifice. I also offer the opinion that marriage is not a constitutional issue or right and that our society fails with its emphasis on the individual rather than the group.

I also offer justification for the independent lawyer in our society, which is largely dominated by the large firm and corporate legal culture. Finally, I conclude that the second failure of the capitalist system at the present time is that we do not live in a free market system. Our market is dominated by major corporations and, in some sense, is monopolistic.

Again, in these essays, I offer questions and suggest answers and do truly desire not that everyone agrees with what I say here, but that everyone derives some benefit and intellectual stimulation from reading these essays. I also welcome comments and criticism to everything I write and offer to the general public or to whoever may chance to read this book.

Chapter 42
Why Capitalism Is a Failed Idea: Part II

In my previous book, *Essays on the Christian World View and Others Political, Literary, and Philosophical,* I posited in my essay "Why Capitalism is a Failed Idea" that the capitalistic system had serious and significant defects and, for want of a better word, failings. I said in that essay that capitalism, in its present form as based on competitiveness, greed, and survival of the fittest, fails as an economic system and even as a philosophical or moral system, since it cuts out and excises a large percentage of people who are given no chance at all because of their race, economic status, and even their health. Capitalism fails to provide sharing and equality, but rewards brute strength and wealth acquisition as the method and goal of the society. I said in this essay that, in many ways, socialism is a better moral or economic system since it equalizes wealth and eliminates classes. I concluded in that essay that a mixed system of socialism and capitalism would be the solution to a more equal, just, and better society for all.

In this present essay, I would like to point out other factors in our present society that make capitalism a failed concept and economic system. It has been propagandized that, in fact, there is a free market in the United States, and so, it is said, there is equal opportunity for all and equal chances. I do not think, at the present time, it is true that, in fact, the so called free market is at all free and open to all. We have experienced a significant concentration of wealth in the United States through mergers of companies.

Thus, independent hardware stores have been eliminated to be substituted by Home Depot. Independent stationary stores have been replaced by Staples. Independent drug stores have been replaced by Rite Aid and CVS. Even, to some extent, independent restaurants have been replaced by chains such as Ruby Tuesday, Taco Bell, etc. Thus, the ability to establish, independently, a successful business in this so called free market is extremely difficult. Even doctors no longer find it easy to establish their own medical practices, and most join HMO's. Lawyers, although many have their own practices, are faced with competition from major law firms that dominate the legal field and, for one reason or another, have obtained all the business clients. Thus, the notion or idea that we have a free market I do not believe to be at all true. We have increasingly, in the United States, an economic system where through mergers more and more businesses are concentrated in fewer and fewer hands.

I say this that capitalism is a failed idea not only, as I said in my first essay conceptually and philosophically, but also practically, since in reality we do not live in a capitalistic system. Rather, the truth of the matter is that we live in a plutocratic and oligarchic system where true competition is significantly stifled by the major corporate sector, or at least, there is a significant attempt to do so.

Capitalism is a failed idea because, as based in its roots on greed and wealth acquisition, it is wrong, and second, it is quite simply no longer functional. The media may promulgate the myth of the free market, but that market is no longer free. Capitalism has failed because it is wrong; it is not a true and valid idea, and, more to the point, the capitalistic system that formerly gave some equal chances to all does not do so any more.

Chapter 43
The Decline of the American Middle Class

When I was a young person living in Bayside Queens, one of my neighbors was a taxi driver who had a non-working wife, and the other was a plumber. My father was a lawyer who worked for the Law Department of the City of New York. We all saw ourselves as members of the American middle class. The fact of the matter is, and I did not know this at that time, that we all considered ourselves as middle class, although frankly, we did not have much money and by today's standards, we were poor. Nevertheless, the taxi driver and plumber owned fairly nice houses and, in all instances, the husbands had non-working wives and several children on what was, by today's standards, rather meager incomes.

Today, by all standards, those persons on my block in Bayside who were members of the middle class are no longer so. This little essay proposes to examine what happened to the middle class in the present day, 2011. I am not an economist or historian, and my knowledge of what happened here is fairly limited. But what I think happened is the following:

Before the Great Depression in 1929 and/or 1930, American society consisted basically of the haves and have-nots. The have-nots at that time were the rural poor. In fact, the United States at that time was probably 60-65% rural and rural poverty was very great, particularly in the South, or at least I think so. The reforms of Franklin D. Roosevelt resulted, by the end of his Presidency, in the creation of an American middle class.

How did this happen? There are several factors. First, after a great struggle, the American worker was permitted to form unions and engage in collective bargaining with the result that the workers in the manufacturing sector were raised, through negotiation and collective bargaining with the manufacturing companies which employed them, to middle class status. At the beginning of this process, the corporate sector vehemently opposed the formation of unions, even to the extent of engaging in violence against them and their formation.

Second, President Roosevelt modified and reformed the raw-boned capitalist system, bringing about such changes as Social Security for persons over 65, Social Security Disability for ill and disabled persons, unemployment insurance for fired or laid off workers, worker's compensation, and others. One of his great projects and reforms was the formation of the Tennessee Valley Authority, which brought electricity to significantly impoverished sections of the rural South. At that time, most of the poverty-stricken rural population of this country probably had no electricity or running water. By 1948 or 1950, after the end of World War II, an American middle class emerged.

That American middle class is not only on the decline, but is in the process of elimination from the scene. The reasons for this are the following factors: 1) unions have been eliminated since the mid-1960s with the result that those workers who obtained middle class status have been pushed down, for want of a better phrase, to the lower economic section of society; 2) there has been an outsourcing of business to Asia, together with an influx of extremely cost effective, if not cheap, Hispanic or Third World labor, who work at extremely low wages, with which the American worker is unable to compete.

Finally, a situation has been created by the global corporate sector to create a peonage system of work within the United States in which workers have no job security, obtain no pensions, and have an extremely limited working life. Often these workers are eliminated from the workforce by the time they are in their mid-forties.

This labor system is extremely cost-effective for the corporate global sector. In fact, for some time now, there have been forces in American society that wish to eliminate Social Security, Medicare, or Medicaid. Thus, the American middle class created by the New Deal has largely been marginalized, if not completely eliminated. Thus, our society has once again been transformed to the prior 1930 society of haves and have-nots. Perhaps the most defined reason for this entire situation is greed, avarice, and selfishness on the part of some small group of people who want as much as they can get and oppose some degree of equal distribution of wealth.

I think, unfortunately, our system, with its gross emphasis on money at its root and core, has brought this situation about. That emphasis on money has pushed out any other thought systems, whether the church, communism, or socialism, which in prior times had some play in the system. All systems are defective because the human beings who participate in them are imperfect. I think the imperfection in our present system lies in its present emphasis on making money the sole yardstick and measuring rod. This is corruption and I speculate it is dragging all of us down.

There is no middle class at this point of juncture in time because there are forces in American society that do not want it. What the future will bring I cannot say, and perhaps I will not live to see it. I can only say that a society solely based on wealth acquisition goes nowhere.

Chapter 44
A Word on American Culture

American culture, in its present form, is problematica. There was at time when poets such as Shelley, Byron, Tennyson, and Browning had a wide audience in the English-speaking world. As well, John Stuart Mill, an English 19th century philosopher, had a wide intellectual impact on the English-speaking world and was even in the House of Commons at one point. In short, writers, poets, and philosophers at one time generated great respect and a substantial public following. Even in the 20th century, philosophers such as John Dewey and Bertrand Russell had a great public impact. These persons, in some ways, were the celebrities of their time.

It is apparent that times have altered and changed, and one may wonder if the change has been for the good. American society has admiration for and sets up on a pedestal, the wealthy, the rich and the famous. For some time now, it has been pounded into the psyches and minds of the American public, that persons with wealth, notoriety, and celebrity fame are the ones to whom we should look up. Images of the rich and famous are constantly flashed for us by way of television images, computer images, and the silver screen. The American public has been propagandized into believing that the rich and famous are the persons to be admired and respected. This is absolutely ridiculous. In our society, little respect is given to intellectual activity, whether scientific or otherwise. The American people are told to respect money and success.

In the early 20th century, Albert Schweitzer left his post in France as a theologian and expert on Bach to serve, for no money reward, African natives in what was then French Africa. He did so because of his Christian commitment to alleviate suffering. It is possible that in today's world, he would be ignored and the public eye, as it is now, would be focused on Donald Trump and Mayor

Blumberg. For every rich and famous celebrity, there is a humble doctor saving lives, a farmer raising food for the world; and, one may hope, a lawyer bringing some form of justice to his clients. For every celebrity and for every one of the rich and famous whose images appear on television and newspapers, there is a mission post throughout the world in which believing Christians render free medical care and establish free schooling for persons too poor to get that help. One may conclude that being rich and famous does not mean a great deal.

Thus, I suggest that American culture, which elevates fame, money and riches, is a poor culture. There is no respect in America for a great writer who earns no money. There is great respect for sports figures and actors and actresses who do. In American society, success is the benchmark and keystone. How one dresses, for an American, defines that person.

In my opinion, American culture is shallow and deficient in its thrust and meaning. Culture should be defined by artistic, intellectual, scientific, and literary contribution and not by wealth, appearance, looks, or the images of success that the media impose on the American public and propagandize into believing their validity and truth. Times change.

In the 4th century A.D., wealthy people went into the desert of Egypt to find Christ. In today's world, people seek to find what they wish will define themselves in their Lexus, or their house in the Hamptons, or their penthouse on Park Avenue. It remains to be seen where the truth lies. One may only say that a Galilean peasant 2,000 years ago founded a movement that is followed by two billion people today. One may wonder whether the wealth and success that American pop culture idolizes will last beyond the deaths of the persons who have presented to us in their lifetimes images that are fictional and false and have no truth.

Chapter 45
What Is a Woman: Feminine or Otherwise

The status of women in western society, and perhaps in all societies, has been something of a problem or issue. Most societies are patriarchal and, therefore, how women function or behave has been defined by the male-dominated power structure. Therefore, men wish women to be feminine, that is to say gentle, kind, and compassionate. Perhaps the reasons for this insistence is that men wish to see in women the image of their mother perhaps, or they wish to dominate by insisting on these qualities in the women around them. The particular qualities I have mentioned: gentleness, kindness, and compassion, I do not think are confined to or are solely the province to the female sex. These qualities are equally distributed in both sexes and their emergence and dispersion depend on the individual person, man or woman. Thus I think compassion and humanity may be found as much in a particular man or a particular woman. Thus the quality of being "feminine" or feminist can be found in either sex. Thus there are men who are football players, boxers, soldiers, and there are men who are poets and artists. I would like to consider in this essay what I think are qualities which are particularly found or attached to the female sex.

I think it is fair to say that, because women bear children and have the responsibility for caring for their children and husband and taking care of the home, that nurturing or functioning as a mother are particularly female qualities. That is not to exclude a man who may be nurturing and may be able to maintain a home and family and raise children. I do think, however, that women are more attuned to this function, whether genetically or culturally.

I would like to indicate what I think are particular female qualities. Of course, depending on the man, many men would wish to see women as feminine and weak, and a fair number wish to perceive the female sex in solely sexual terms and no other. Thus it is an unfortunate, but hard, fact that pornography and prostitution appeal solely to the male sex, with some exceptions. In fact this has been true for some thousands of years. Cave paintings and many artistic productions, because they are done by men, depict naked women because that is the way men like to see women depicted: purely in sexual terms. Female sexuality, in that sense as depicted by men, is completely erroneous and wrong. It is the projection of what men want to see in a woman. Thus femininity and outright female sexuality as depicted in pornography and paintings are not female qualities.

The quality of nurturing may be a female quality, but I am not sure whether in fact it is cultural. I do say this, however, about what I think constitutes female qualities. Women, despite what people may say in the modern world, wish to have families, homes, and husbands. What emerges from that decision are what I think are genetically defined as female qualities. These qualities are 1) love, 2) devotion, and 3) sacrifice. They involve a degree of pain and, more exactly involve the subsuming of the mother's personality and goals to the needs of her children and husband. Women marry, although they may deny it, to give love to their connected husband and children. This involves a lifetime of devotion to the husband and children and great sacrifice.

My observation of how things are in this respect, concerning what constitutes female qualities, leads me the conclusion that eroticism and feminism are cultural qualities imposed by the patriarchy or male power structure. What I think are defined female qualities found only in women are the love, devotion, and sacrifice that only occur in the family structure and manifest themselves in marriage to the husband provider and the birth and nurturing of children.

I would like to add what I think is another female quality, not quite as prevalent as it has been. That quality is the desire of the woman to please. A woman who lacks the quality or ability to please, I think, may have a deficit or lack of that particular quality.

I say this finally: the overarching female quality that I think is attached to being a woman is interest in the person rather than the subject. This particular quality of personal interest, attachment, or devotion to the person is a basic female quality that men may lack in their role of workers and providers in the business world.

To conclude, what I think are the alleged female qualities of compassion, kindness, and gentleness are equally distributed in both sexes, depending on the person. There are surely as many kind and compassionate men as there are kind and compassionate women. Perhaps because women wish to see strength and aggression in men, they conclude these qualities of compassion, kindness, and gentleness are barred from the male personality. If that is so, they are obviously wrong and incorrect. By the same token, because men wish to see women as feminine and gentle, they may exclude the qualities of strength and aggression from their expression in women. Again. aggression and strength are not con-fined to either sex and, as a matter of fact, to be a mother and maintain a home and children require great strength and aggression.

I conclude this little essay by saying the following: devotion, sacrifice, and love, as well as the desire and act of pleasing, are qualities found mostly in women, and these qualities emanate from the female interest and attachment to the person and personal as opposed to the world of business and abstract thought.

Chapter 46
A Word on the Digital Age

For some time now, ever since the advent of television in the late 1940's, print as the primary mode of mass communication has experienced a severe decline publicly. At one time there were many, many newspapers, expressing many different viewpoints, including the Communist newspaper, *The Daily Worker.* Many, many viewpoints and opinions were expressed in these dailies. With the coming of television, computers, the Internet, DVDs, VCRs, iPods, camcorders, cell phones, text messages, e-mails, and other myriad forms of speedy communication, print as the primary expression of mass communication and thought has taken a back seat.

Although many books are published, I think people read less although I cannot be sure of this. In addition we are constantly bombarded with a succession of images where politicians, rock stars, entertainers, sports figures, or various celebrities are currently in—or are thrust temporarily into—the public's eye.

I think there are two effects of these developments. First, with speed and a constant bombardment of images comes the inability to focus and concentrate. The person's mind is distracted and, in a sense, loses the ability to discern detail and thought on an exact and critical basis. In addition, speed, which we have been compelled to adapt as a society, may result in more production but less quality and less thought. Thus images and speed distract and perhaps confuse. Not only does this speed and image bombardment result in the inability to focus and concentrate, but they give way or room for the big lie or, better part, propaganda.

When the public sees an image, but know nothing of it, and this image is thus faster and faster and more constantly on the person's mind and consciousness, that person will be confused and unable to discern wherein lies the truth.

Many politicians claim to write books. I cannot say whether they are the authors or not, but they are making a representation to that effect. The problem occurs when a constant succession of mindless expressions is cast on the public, the truth is hidden, and lies are accomplished. The lie can be so convincing that a terrorist will kill and commit suicide for Islam. The lie can be so massive as to convince the public that money, greed, materialism, and raw power are actual value and should be respected. Truth can be covered up by lies: lies about persons in the public eye, lies not admitting meritorious persons to the public eye, lies featuring whomever the lie wants to feature and what the lie wants to say.

It is important for us all as a society to let the truth, which is often hidden, emerge in thoughtful, discerning books presented by knowledgeable persons who have something to say. The book will always be able to present truth that speed images and blaring noise will always successfully hide. It is imperative that our society return not only to the printed word, the product of careful thought, but return to the books which having been vetted by time which will always serve to inform and enlighten, whether the Bible, Shakespeare, Dante or Milton. Having survived the passage of time, these books contain truths that noise and speed cannot hide. We eliminate books at our peril. Lies led to racist lynchings. Lies, said often enough and frequently enough, make people slaves, create false class distinctions, justify the Hitlers, Stalins, Pol Pots, and Putins, and make fools of us all.

Chapter 47
The Money Culture

The present system in the United States, and in many parts of the world, might
be termed free market capitalism. The capitalist economic system is based on
acquisition and greed. The idea behind it is that if all of us are given some sort
of equal starting point in a free market economy, businesses will be created, jobs
created, and society materially advanced. This system maintains the notion that
a person with a particular concept or idea is given the chance in this system to
build a business on the basis of that idea. The idea can take the form of a Star-
bucks or Kentucky Fried Chicken. Behind the capitalist system also lie the idea
or concept that if people are given the motivation of greed to advance themselves materially, the entire society benefits by creating jobs, producing goods,
offering services, and spending money to purchase those goods and services.

Many people argue that socialism and communism have been tried and
failed. The last communist bastions are Cuba and North Korea. Both are impoverished social and economic systems. I am not sure whether capitalism is the
best system but I think it should be regulated, since it results in great inequities
of wealth and the creation and continuance of class structures. I would suggest
that socialism has its points since it eliminates class, attempts to equalize wealth,
and provides free schooling and jobs for all within that system. As I said, however, socialism and communism have been shown to be not particularly successful social or economic systems.

In this essay, I find two faults with the capitalist system. Better put, I find
greed and money as the sole aims and bases of life defective. First, when money
and greed and procurement of things for oneself are made the sole objectives,

the entire society is degraded. In their desire for money, persons may not care about their work or what they are doing. Many simply aim to get as much money and do as little as they can. Thus there may be doctors who are solely focused on money and have no particular commitment to their patients or their profession. The same may be true of lawyers.

In fact, where the sole desire and object of the occupation or task is money, degradation and disintegration occur. Thus, we all know, that we may go to an auto mechanic and routinely be told we need a brake job, a new transmission, a new battery. There is a good chance that the mechanic has simply taken the easy path of making the consumer spend a fairly large sum of money without the mechanic's having taken the time, trouble, and work to find out what is actually wrong with the car.

This corruption and outright fraud connected with the desire for money take a number of forms in our present society. That form may be the imposition of excessive charges on the part of the professional or business person when that person well knows that minimal or little work is actually involved. Our politicians regularly say they write books. It is possible that they do so, and I make no claim that they do not, but knowing the difficulty of the task of producing a book, the politician's claim to have done so is somewhat questionable.

One may think, possibly, that many books that are produced by notable figures, whether politicians, movie stars, or sports figures, are not actually produced by their own efforts, although this cannot be actually proved but only questioned. Most of us know that to do a 300- or 400-page book is an extremely laborious and time consuming effort. Again, one can only conclude that the desire for money and fame often has brought about this particular situation and phenomenon. Thus, one deficit of a money culture such as ours, focused on greed and acquisition, is that not only is the work product degraded but the object of the person's effort, which should be to produce something which is of benefit to society, is substituted and cancelled, downgraded to getting as much money as one can.

In some sense, when money is the only consideration, our society not only is pulled down, but the intellectual underpinnings of our system are brought to nothing. Our system seems to be telling people that as long as you make money, that is all that counts. The system also says that what is not connected with money is of no value. This would include buying a Bible for $5.00 as opposed to purchasing a Lexus for $35,000.00. When money is the only object and greed the sole purpose, we are all told that whatever good we may do in our lives counts for nothing.

I have a second criticism of our money and greed culture. When money is made the sole criterion and benchmark, there will not and cannot be any love. If people are seen only as economic commodities, love is out the window. In a relationship based on money, where either partner, man or woman, chooses their husband or wife on the basis of wealth, there cannot be love in that relationship.

In short, I am most convinced that a materialistic money culture is destructive of any chance for love in that system.

Love can only be found where something else occurs besides wealth, money, or the acquisition of something out of that other person for yourself. The capitalistic culture taken to its extreme extent based on money and greed destroys and eradicates any chance for love in a society in which people are desperately seeking it through online dating, personal advertisements, and casual sexual encounters.

Chapter 48
Why We Need Lawyers

The legal profession in the United States, and in most parts of the world, largely consists, first, of very large law firms which are composed of a fairly large number of partners and an even larger number of associates and, secondly, of businesses which have in-house legal counsel. These firms and corporate counsel function to service the extremely large business sectors of the world. The associates in these firms function to produce billable hours at a very large hourly rate of perhaps between $200 and $500 per hour to create profits for the law firms which submit these bills to their business clients. The partners in these law firms have become so largely through the investment of money in the firm, through a family or business connection, or through their ability to bring in corporate clients.

In fact, not only may they not be particularly talented or good lawyers, but that particular quality is not required since they are in those very large law firms for one of the reasons I indicated. The partners in these law firms and corporate counsel as well, one could say, obtain government positions of a substantive character at times. In short, there may be a kind of power or money exchange between corporations, government, and very large law firms. Thus, most of the legal profession consists of this group of lawyers.

There is one other group of lawyers, much smaller in number, who have far less power than the law firms and corporate counsel I have just spoken of. These are independent lawyers, in their own firms, of their own creation, who seek to represent individuals and enforce their rights. Since these lawyers do not have large corporate or firm backing, for these lawyers to be successful requires some degree of ability, since, to put it bluntly, they are not getting any help from large numbers of paralegals and associates, and they may not have a great deal of money.

These other lawyers we need and the world needs. These other lawyers, such as Thurgood Marshall, help bring about a better and more just society by taking on unpopular clients and unpopular causes. For every corporate lawyer and partner in a big law firm, there is an individual practitioner who represents an indigent criminal. These lawyers seek to equalize the society and perhaps provide a chance for people lacking in funds to gain a foothold in the system that they might not otherwise have.

The world system and the world power structure are stacked against these lawyers. They represent interests and persons whom most people would not like to admit are not only without funds or standing in the world, but quite frankly, are mostly despised. No one would like to say this, but the world respects money and power and does not particularly give respect to those persons who are not in that class of persons or in that system. The world desperately needs independent lawyers who are willing to challenge traditions that should be changed and injustices that should be corrected.

There was a time when women could not vote and African Americans had no rights. No doubt, at that time, the society resisted these people's having a place in the system. Those same power structures that resisted those groups' gaining their rights and opportunities in the system resist different groups of people, in different ways, in today's world.

The only hope for disenfranchised persons, lacking wealth and not having much in material goods or social standing, is this group of independent lawyers who, by great effort and in the face of great resistance, stand up for people with whom society declines to share. These lawyers give those persons a chance they might not otherwise have, and by giving a chance to those persons, things can happen in our system and society that we might never dream of.

The persons who have money may get into medical school and make a lot of money, but if these persons I have just described get into medical school, the next step will be a cure for cancer or a vaccine for Alzheimer's. Lawyers who are unconnected with the world power structure can bring about changes to our society that might never happen.

We need independent lawyers because they are the only hope for most of the world that the world system wants to shut out.

Chapter 49
A Crisis in Culture

At the present time, our culture is in crisis. Let me say that in certain areas there have been significant advances such as in technology and medicine. The fact of the matter is, however, what we may define as culture in terms of literature, poetry, philosophy, drama, painting, and certain types of music have come to an end. This is a rather obvious fact. During the Twentieth Century, there was outstanding dramatic production in both the American and English theater. Playwrights such as George Bernard Shaw, Tennessee Williams, Eugene ONeill, Arthur Miller, Clifford Odets, and Lillian Hellman come to mind.

Live dramatic productions have ceased and one can speculate have been replaced by television and movies. At one time, and rather recently in the Nineteenth Century, there was a very large public audience for poetry. The most recent Twentieth Century poets to have that public audience were T.S. Elliot and William Butler Yeats. Poetry, as an artistic medium of expression directed to the wider public no longer exists. It is obvious that painting and sculpture are essentially passé, apparently replaced by other forms of imagery such as television, movies, and camera images. The novel still survives, but not as it appeared in the Nineteenth Century in its more complex expression and structure in such novels as *Middlemarch* by George Eliot and *War and Peace* by Tolstoy.

It is also quite apparent that classical music has had its day, last heard by such composer as Richard Strauss and Igor Stravinsky. One may say that the American musical theater from 1930 to 1955 or 1960 was a further expression of that classical musical impulse. At the present time, even that type of musical expression is gone. Most musicals on the Broadway stage today consist of a redoing of the older musicals.

The question that comes to mind is why many forms of art have ceased to exist, in effect, and appeal to a very miniscule audience. I suggest two reasons for his. There has been a decline in religious belief and the Church has very little influence on the wider culture as it once did. The rhythms and drama and stories in the Bible are presently unfamiliar to a large percentage, if not most, of the population. When a society has no spiritual underpinning, one can only conclude that the expression of art and beauty will cease. A purely materialistic society such as now obtains in the Western world cannot produce art and express beauty. This is speculation, I say, but I believe there is some truth to it. We may have computers and all sorts of gadgetry, but apparently we cannot produce the Bachs or Mozarts or the Miltons or the Dantes. We do things faster but we fail to reach people in the souls. It is also significant that philosophy is no longer a part of our society in the way it once was. Two important American thinkers of the last century come to mind: John Dewey and William James. Philosophy today has only an academic audience, if any.

I proffer a second reason for this cultural decline. The education offered in the Western world is no longer literary as it once was. There is an overwhelming emphasis on money and business, even in the educational system. When people no longer are given the literary past and have it made available to them, their minds will suffer and deteriorate in the areas I just mentioned. Reading great books of literature raises the mind to the ability to think creatively and artistically. When the system does not give our young people this food for their minds, again, I thing the type of artistic productions I mentioned will not occur.

A final word. Many people will say that as long as I have the material goods I need and I can pay my expenses, that is all I need. The purpose of life, however, is to raise people beyond that essential and basic level of functioning. A society without music, literature, poetry, and art must be a very gray and dark society; that society that at the present time we all have to suffer in. A society without art and beauty must create and bring about a very unhappy race of beings whose lives are most somber and lack deep meaning, depth and, in fact, lack love.

A society without art and without beauty is a society without love and surely without God.

Chapter 50
A Word on Work

In our present society, many people make much of, or rather pin their sense of importance on, the work that they do. Work may generally be defined as how any one person may earn their living to pay whatever expenses and financial obligations they may have. Nevertheless, many people make much of their work and define their self and self importance by whatever they do to earn a living. Thus it would appear that professionals such as lawyers, doctors, accountants, and many businessmen or executives feel a sense of greater worth or superiority in terms of the work they are doing or may do.

In fact, in the world there are two kinds of work, I think. One is work which involves a more physical aspect or components such as a policeman, a fireman, a plumber, or a carpenter. These occupations and types of work are somewhat incorrectly defined as "blue collar." Blue collar work also includes farmers, electricians, and military personnel. The second type of work in the world is work which is defined by more mental, or perhaps written, activity. As I said, this group of "white collar" workers includes those in such occupations as lawyers, doctors, academics, and all sorts of teachers.

For some reasons, there are groups, or forces rather, within our society that define these white collar, or for want of a better word, more intellectual occupations as giving them a superior position in society. It is almost as if a professional, who does less with his hands and more with his head and more with telephone conversations, letters, and e-mails, is defined by many people as upper or higher class because of their particular work. Perhaps it is because they wear a suit and go to an office building that our society defines these people as high class as opposed to their blue collar brothers whose work is more manual or physical.

This thinking, I suggest, is erroneous and incorrect. Work in terms of physical work or activity is no less significant or important than the white collar work that lawyers, doctors, or executives do. Thus farmers grow all our food. Those who say that the work of a lawyer is more important than that of a farmer are clearly and absolutely incorrect. No one in this world can survive for one day without farmers. We might more easily do without executives or lawyers for a number of days.

The same is true of military personnel who defend their country against foreign invaders or attack or the bus driver who takes people to their destination safely and intact. In fact, all occupations are equally important and equally necessary. Our entire system and society is interdependent on every occupation and work that any one person may do. It is an intellectual error and an essential act of arrogance to make the office worker or executive higher class than the firefighter or policeman who risk their lives on a daily basis and save lives on a daily basis.

It is somewhat puzzling that our society raises these white collar occupations to some sort of class status in our society. I very much fear that this is the case and it is rather foolish to come to this conclusion when we all know that none of us can do one day without the police, one day without the firefighter, or even a day without sanitation collection. The fact that there are various types of work in our society cannot lead anyone who has given the matter any thought to the conclusion that because there are different types of jobs or different types of work that anyone is more important or less essential. Perhaps it is almost an act of defective human nature to label blue collar or physical work as of somewhat less significance than the while collar work I have mentioned.

In a sense there is basically no difference and no distinction. I have heard the term "working class" used. The word is a class status or class definitional statement. To attach these labels to blue collar or physical occupations is to denigrate and pull down work that is, perhaps, more important and more significant that what our CEO's are paid millions of dollars to do.

When a fireman saves lives and a military person defends us against people who threaten our society, the word "class" as attached to those activities begs the question.

Chapter 51
Was Marx Right?

For some time now, many countries and societies have adopted the capitalist model or system. Communism has essentially collapsed in most of the world, with the exception of North Korea and Cuba. Unfortunately, the capitalist system has evolved to a somewhat deficient end. Capitalism is based on greed and competition and on a free market system. The idea behind it is that if that if people are given some sort of an equal starting point, the society will benefit by job creation and wealth creation and all will benefit ultimately. Capitalism, however, has developed in a somewhat more negative direction than originally envisioned.

There are many reasons for this development. Jobs have been outsourced to South America and Asia. Unions in the United States have largely been eliminated; there has been a significant influx of cheap labor from South America and Asia to the United States; in the name of supply side economics, there has been a vast transfer of wealth to an extremely small segment of the population in the United States. Manufacturing has largely left the United States for places where the labor pool is inexpensive, such as Asia and South America.

The result of these developments has been threefold. It has been very difficult for the American worker to get employment. The jobs that do exist are without benefits such as pensions or health benefits. Older workers are easily—and constantly—dispensed with for younger workers. The end outcome of all these developments is to make it extremely difficult for any American worker to obtain some sort of quality employment to support his family for as long as needed. The end result, in another way, is to create a plutocratic and oligarchic system where the economic and political structures are controlled by a few wealthy individuals and corporations. In short, the capitalist system has become extremely unfair and functions now to exclude people from opportunities to advance themselves or even to enter the economic and political system. It would appear that the capitalist system is in crisis and has become dysfunctional.

This essay proposes that Marx may have been right. Marx and Engels responded, in their writings and activities, to the abuses of the working class in industrialized countries in Europe at that time. These abuses included child labor and the use of sweat shop labor. Marxism proposes a number of ideas and concepts which I think are good. 1) It eliminates class divisions which capitalism encourages. These class divisions are falsely based on some persons' having greater wealth than others. It is faintly ridiculous to refer to a person who has greater wealth than others in this society as upper class, since the having of wealth has no significance. 2) Marxism seeks to provide some sort of employment for all and provides free healthcare and free education for the entire population. Eliminating income inequality allows people of talent and merit the possibility of obtaining positions that the capitalist society might bar them from based on their lack of wealth. The ultimate aim of Marx in his writings was to bring about a society not controlled by the wealthy or aristocracy, but by the workers. Unfortunately, in various countries such as Russia, China, Cuba, and North Korea, attempts to bring about these potentially good things resulted in the use of force and a totalitarian state or dictatorship.

In sum, Marx had some ideas and concepts that still have value and should be considered by thinking people. 1) The elimination of classes is a good thing; 2) the elimination of income inequality and the redistribution of wealth is also a good thing; and 3) certainly that a society should be governed by the people is a good thing. I cannot say where Marx or Marxism went wrong but, at the present time, the capitalist system as it has developed and evolved is problematic and wanting. The capitalist system has evolved into a sort of totalitarian state in which the wealthy elite rule and in which the vast majority of the population toil to survive. I cannot give a solution to the present difficulties in our system, but I can say this much: that the system should be reexamined in the light of the ideas behind Marxism and socialism. This is not say that I wish to impose a totalitarianism society which Marxist society developed into, but I do suggest that the present state of the capitalist system should be reexamined in light of other concepts, thoughts, and ideas wherever they may be found.

Chapter 52
Marriage Equality

One of the hot button topics of public discourse and discussion of late has been the issue of same-sex marriage or marriage between homosexuals as opposed to being solely limited to heterosexuals. First, let me note that certain religious groups such as the Orthodox Jews, the Roman Catholic Church, the Orthodox Church, the Islamic community, and certain conservative Protestant Christian denominations reject on a moral basis or religious/ethical basis the concept of same-sex marriage.

This essay does not touch upon the religious issue. The present issue is whether in the political/social system same-sex marriage should be made legal. For some hundreds of years, marriage has been seen as the union between men and women to establish homes and families, to provide an environment for bringing children into the world which will bring them into society equipped to function, and also to hand down property to the next generation. Marriage has also been seen as a method or means of protecting women and children from the possibility of abuse. When women were economically dependent, they were provided with shelter and the means for survival by the breadwinner husband. The issue today has been defined as "marriage equality." The meaning and implication in this terminology is that other forms of marriage other than heterosexual marriage involve some sort of constitutional entitlement or right. This, in my view, is a mistake, a misapprehension, and has the wrong meaning. I do not tackle the issue here whether same-sex marriage is a good thing, whether there should be laws against it, or wither the law should permit it and encourage it. In this essay, I do not touch upon those particular issues.

Marriage in the United States and other countries has not been regulated by the national government and certainly has no connection with the United States

Constitution, the Bill of Rights, or the Equal Protection or Due Process clauses of the United States Constitution. In the United States, marriage has been regulated and established by the states and local governments, whether cities or counties. Like education in the United States, marriage and education have been left to the individual states and localities to be established and regulated. Therefore the idea behind the phrase "marriage equality" is a misnomer.

In the United States the word "equality" is constantly spoken of, bandied about, and made a societal goal in the social system. It is certainly a good thing that in the political system, that is to say in the one-man-one vote system, there is equality. It is also a good thing that there is a classless system or social equality in the United States. Most certainly there is a spiritual quality attached to all men and women as individuals before God. Of course, people are not equal in their talents and abilities.

The point I take here is that to use the term "marriage equality" with respect to same-sex marriage is an attempt to invest some sort of constitutional right or protection to same-sex marriage. Since the Constitution and the idea of equality have no connection with same-sex marriage, the use of the term "marriage equality' is puzzling and misleading.

That group or those individuals who believe in same-sex marriage in the civil society and political system certainly have the right to have and to promote their views in this respect. However, I must and do say that the term "equality" attached to the marriage relationship raises the idea that marriage involves some sort or form of constitutional protection or right in this particular situation.

In short, I do not believe that the United States Constitution or the Equal Protection clause of the United State Constitution have anything to do with same-sex marriage or so called "marriage equality." Of course those who use the term may simply be using the term "equal" with respect to every activity or relationship in our society, including marriage.

I end by saying, however, that marriage is a state of local regulation and furthermore the Constitution of this country with its goal of affording equal treatment under the law to all citizens has nothing to do with this issue. It is not a matter of equality under our constitutional system, but whether marriage in this form should be allowed and regulated by the states and localities as marriage always has been and presently is.

Chapter 53
Why We Need Unions: A Reprise

In a previous book of mine entitled *Essays on a Christian World View and Others*, I wrote a short essay, "Why We Need Unions." In that essay I argued that since workers lack power, or rather a balance of power with respect to their employers, unions are necessary and enable workers to obtain an essentially middle class standard of living.

Recently over four hundred workers in two recent fires at Asian garment factories, which manufacture clothes for European and American brands, died. The accounts of these fires in Bangladesh and Pakistan seemed to indicate that there were few, if any, safety standards present, that the owners of both factories had barred windows to prevent theft, and that there were no usable safety fire exits.

Although one can argue that the lack of safety standards and safe fire exits are the reasons for the deaths of these workers, the more exact reason is that those countries probably do not have or permit unionization of workers. *The New York Times* in an editorial dated December 10, 2012, noted correctly what had happened. To analyze the situation more closely one can speculate that these garment factories in which workers lacked union protection and lacked safety mechanisms are the result of the outsourcing of jobs to third world countries which use third world labor at a fraction of the cost we pay to Americans. This outsourcing essentially caused this tragedy. There have been efforts made by labor groups in these companies to establish union and there has been great difficulty in that area and opposition to that movement. Labor organizers have even been murdered in their efforts to improve working conditions for third world workers.

This particular tragedy and others in Bangladesh and Pakistan demonstrate that when unions are not permitted to be established to protect workers in their jobs and working conditions, this will be the result. It is unfortunate that many businesses which are only and completely after profits will oppose unions in order to continue to gain greater profits through the cheap labor force in these third world countries where people are desperate for any sort of employment.

It is a travesty that the American people should buy goods from these counties over the burned and murdered bodies of persons who are desperate for any kind of income to survive. Unions, if permitted would put a stopgap on these sorts of horrible tragedies. More to the point, can the American people, or any person in good conscience, purchase goods manufactured over the dead and burned carcasses of their fellow human beings? The issue here is, more exactly, shall we and should we permit and continue profits to be made over the sufferings and deaths of other human beings?

The author is indebted in part in the language of this article to *The New York Times* editorial on December 10, 2012, entitled "Fire Safety in Garment Factories." A 26.

Chapter 54
Another Word about Feminism

In a previous essay in a book entitled *Essays on the Christian World View*, I wrote an essay entitled "The Feminist Movement: A Critique." In that essay I of course agreed wholeheartedly with the feminist movement that women, as members of the human race, should have full job opportunities. The society would suffer if any group, whether women or men of whatever race, class or religion, were excluded from obtaining the kind of work they want and developing themselves and hopefully contributing to society in that particular position.

I noted that one fault, if you could call it that, of the women's movement was to wrongly imitate what was thought to be traditional male characteristics such as hardness, the cutting edge, domination, and aggressiveness. As I said in that essay, I see these as human qualities, qualities equally distributed to male and female but certainly not the best human qualities. Lack of feeling, toughness, and callousness, I said in that essay, are certainly not worthy of imitation by either sex. I would like to say something more her about what I see as a negative outcome or result of feminism.

Before the feminist movement, women were in a more dependent relationship to men, or better put, may have taken care of the home, but the provision for the economic structure of the home and family was traditionally provided by the male. Thus, in some sense, the relationship was inequal. Because of that inequality, abuses in that relationship did occur. The wife and mother may have had no job skills and have been subject to verbal and even physical abuse by the father and husband. I do state here, however, that these is another negative effect or result in his change in the societal structure.

The concept of romantic love has been part of our culture for some thousands of years. When, as in the modern world, there is full equality, that concept must suffer and ultimately end. Romantic love is based on courtship and on raising the woman on a pedestal. It is based, not on male dominance or superiority but on the subtle idea that the woman is to be treasured, respected and made the object of male love and adoration. When the woman in society has achieved full equality in the workplace and in the marriage, although weighing the alternatives this is probably good for us all, nevertheless, romantic love, the subject of love poetry for some hundreds of years must gradually end and be no more.

When the woman is no longer raised up and glorified and taken care of in love by the male provider, but is fully equal, full equality has no role in romance. Romantic love is not based on economic and political quality but on other wellsprings or nature that have nothing to do with politics or economics. I laud the feminist movement and all movements that provide political and economic equality and an equal chance in this system for all of us, whether men or women. I mourn the loss of romance.

If we look at the popular music of the past and the theatre and movies of the past, we see this concept still intact, whether in the love songs of *South Pacific* or the delicate ballroom dancing of Fred Astaire and Ginger Rogers. Full equality is an advance and a good thing but it leaves romance and romantic love forever and, one may speculate, that it may never return, at least in the form it was in our society.

Chapter 55
Some Aspects of American Culture

American culture has many positive attributes and qualities attached to it. For many years, until recently, when other members of other religions, such as Islam and Hinduism, have come to this country, American was regarded by many people in this country as a "Christian society." In some ways, American culture does to some extent have that sort of connection. For example, for American society there is some form of social equality exhibited. Better put, American society functions to some extent without overt class distinctions. That is to say, the less affluent person or poor person is treated in America with the same response as a rich person gains. This social equality may be a façade, but it is certainly better than a class-ridden culture and is closer to the gospel and to the Christian message.

Second, American culture exhibits a certain geniality and acceptance of most other sorts of people, races, cultures, and religions. Again, that geniality and acceptance and non-criticism of others, whoever they may be, is certainly more of a Christian form of behavior than excluding others from the social system based on those factors or attributes. In some sense, this lack of overt class structure in a society and general acceptance of most others as they may present themselves to society probably stems from the obvious political equality in the American system that is based on one man, one vote. That is to say, the vote of the rich man is the same as the poor man in forming the government, whether local, state, or federal.

On the other hand I find certain traits in the American culture counter to Christ, counter to the Christian message, and contrary to the gospel.

American culture is largely based on business and commerce. The entire society is geared toward the acquisition and gaining of materiel wealth through business activity. It is quite obvious that this is not the Christian perspective. It is somewhat hidden in the Christian thought system in today's world, but nevertheless true, that Christianity lays preference on embracing poverty rather than the acquisition of material wealth. Jesus states in the gospel that the poor in spirit, or humble, are blessed. Jesus states that the meek will inherit the earth. He states that it is extremely difficult for a rich man to enter the kingdom of heaven. Hence, the emphasis in American culture on wealth and materialism is obviously not within, and in fact quite the contrary to, the Christian belief system.

When a rich man came to Christ in the gospel and asked what he had to do to be perfect, he was told to give up all his goods. This emphasis on poverty in the Christian belief system is best understood when we realize that in the Roman Catholic Church, monastic orders involve the taking of the vow of poverty. This is also true of the religious orders of men and women, who also take a vow of poverty in the Roman Catholic Church. For many hundreds of year there has been a great movement of people embracing, one might say, this alternative life choice of embracing poverty.

The second aspect of American culture that is very much non-Christian is the phenomenon of advertising and celebrities. The Christian belief system emphasizes humility, not self-importance. Thus, advertising and raising individuals up as celebrities is, in fact, quite contrary and opposed to the Christian belief in humility.

These two latter aspects of the American culture that I have identified as non-Christian probably have their origin in the capitalist commercial system and in the emphasis on money and business. Better put, people in the United States are measured by their success in the market.

Christians measure things and people differently. I make this point only to identify what I think are Christian values that are present in the American system and what I see as non-Christian concepts that I think should be examined by the Church and addressed as not particularly helpful as to how people should function. Perhaps, one may say, to function on the basis of money and advertising is to miss a great deal of ideas and thoughts that could make a better society for us all.

There will never be a Christian society because of the inherent imperfection and dislocation of human nature as a result of sin. That imperfection will never be eradicated except on an individual basis through transformation with a relationship with Christ and his Church. Nevertheless, I do address these particular issues here to point out inherent philosophical failings in American culture that should perhaps be changed, altered, or redirected and reformed.

Chapter 56
Individualism and Collectivism

America, the United States, is said to be the land of promise, the land of opportunity, and the place for individual ideas, initiative, and accomplishment. One might say that the society in this country was founded upon the individual's making his way on his or her own. Whether it was the Puritans, the Pilgrims, the pioneers, or the waves of immigrant groups that came to these shores to seek their fortunes, whether Italians, Irish, Jewish people and now Hispanics, Africans and Asians, the model in this country was that you make it on your own since everybody has an equal chance.

This particular notion or idea did have greater validity in the past when the society in America was more undeveloped, open, and, in a word, there were more opportunities. At one point in our country, anyone who applied to law school—even Columbia Law School—was accepted. Today there is very great and intense competition for admission to top universities and colleges. In fact, up to the end of the 19th Century, the eighth grade education, and then gradually later high school education, was more than sufficient for most people to make their way in life.

The world, however, has vastly changed and I think the idea that if you don't make it, it is your own fault is outdated. Our present society is based on international corporate power and wealth. It is increasingly difficult for the individual to gain a foothold in our system without a great deal of financial help from his family. One might say that we have become a "class-ridden and – driven society." It is extremely unfair to expect a person without a great deal of family means to have the same opportunities and chances as the one with the wealthy background.

The fact of the matter is that we are no longer a 19th Century log cabin country and society. The days when if you worked hard you gained the fruits are not, I think, a viable model anymore. It is extremely unjust to blame the person who is attempting without help by working hard to advance themselves and to say that either that person lacks ability, has not worked hard enough, or cannot compete. I think that persons who say and maintain that are either without experience or wish to pat themselves on the back at the expense of the less fortunate members of society who struggle and are engaged in basic economic survival.

Perhaps the better system would be for the less financially backed member of our system to be given a bit of encouragement and help and not to be told that if you haven't made or don't make it, it is your own fault. The days of the open range are long gone and the days of becoming president and rising from poverty to gain that office are long gone. The myth of individualism that is propagandized to our people is, to put it bluntly, something of a falsehood.

Chapter 57
The Elite

The term "elite" or "the elite" has come into frequent conversation in our society and is a "hot topic." The term usually refers to those persons who have graduated from the top educational institutions, usually Ivy League colleges, and has further reference to those persons who attain power positions, usually by reason of their wealth and background, in the government and business sectors of this country. They are seen as leaders and often seen as the greats by reason of their wealth and status.

It would appear that these person are referred to as "elite" solely by reason of their wealth, privilege, and, to put it rather bluntly, their supposed upper class status in this country. This little essay seeks to correct and name who are really the elites.

The fact of the matter is that wealth in itself has no significance other than making the person who has it, has inherited it, or has acquired it, able to have an easier and more comfortable life. The person who has a degree of wealth is able to acquire more, get more, and possibly gain power and status in our society by reason of their wealth. It is somewhat puzzling that a person having wealth should be regarded as elite. I would ask those same wealthy persons who Jonas Salk, who discovered the polio vaccine, is if not elite. I submit that his status as an "elite" is far beyond the grasp of a person who merely has wealth and nothing more.

I ask, if wealth is the only criteria, where does one place Shakespeare, Tolstoy, and the committee who wrote the King James version of the Bible? If wealth is the sole benchmark, I ask these so-called elite who the elite really are in fact.

Perhaps one might say that for a Christian, wealth has no particular significance in itself. For the Christian, whatever talents we may have, including wealth, should we have it, are gifts of God to be used in the service of others. I do not find wealth and power of particular significance, and so to term a person "elite" because of these accidents is not only puzzling but faintly ridiculous. In fact, the persons who regard someone who has solely wealth and power as "elite" are impoverished in their thinking. For the Christian, and for any right thinking person, people who makes the world a better place during their lives and contribute to society as much as their time and ability permit are the true elite. A great scientist such as Jonas Salk, great writers such as Tolstoy and Shakespeare, and a great religious thinker such as St. Paul are the true elites.

No history book or record can be found that regards wealth as significant in itself, other than that through the ages wealthy people have had the power. Unfortunately those same wealthy people may lack the character and intellect that the person lacking wealth may have and can use to bring something good to the world. For every wealthy person, there is a scientist, a writer, and a thinker who move the world, not devoting their lives solely to themselves but to some other concept, idea, or goal that will bring about something good for us all.

Perhaps one can conclude this essay by saying that the poet who wrote the Twenty-third Psalm and St. Paul who wrote Chapter 13 of his Epistle to the Corinthian Church have done and continue to do for the world what no wealthy person has ever done or can ever attain. St. Paul, perhaps the greatest religious thinker ever known, was kept in chains in Rome and executed by the Roman authorities. Perhaps St. Paul's wealthy counterparts continued to flourish after his death, but again one can ask the question who is elite and who is not.

It is significant that twelve apostles, penniless and having nothing, within 400 years bought about the conversion of the entire Roman Empire. One can only say and ask if the elite are defined by their wealth and class, how does one define the twelve apostles, who virtually brought about a world revolution without funds and without the social status that the modern world so worships and values.

This essay must end by saying that the wealthy and powerful bear no comparison to the true elite of the world whom I have mentioned. To be elite is to be humble. To be elite is to serve others, not to manipulate and get things from others. I can think of no more shallow goal than thinking that obtaining wealth makes one elite. The elite fail to reckon with the Dantes, the Miltons, the Chekovs, with Jesus, Moses, and the authors of the four gospels. It is unfortunate that the elite in our society bear no comparison with those individuals I have mentioned, who in fact have transformed the world.

Chapter 58
A Third Word on the Capitalist System

In two previous essays, one entitled "Why Capitalism Is a Failed Idea" and another in this book entitled "Why Capitalism Is a Failed Idea, Part Two," I examined what I see as a failed capitalist system with its emphasis on greed and
wealth acquisition. I pointed out in part two that we in fact do not live in a free
market at this point but in fact live in a monopolistic or oligarchic system where
the market is run by global business entities. Thus, we have no more independent stationery stores, but Staples, no independent hardware stores, but Home
Depot, and no independent drug stores, but Rite Aid and CVS.

I would like now to offer a third criticism of the capitalist system. Since the
capitalist system is based on wealth acquisition, greed, and money alone, the
result, I think is that the society is transformed into pitting people against each
other on the basis of one person's getting more and outdoing other people. The
result is that the society becomes hostile and divided and seeks to hurt others in
this economic race. I think a better system, if possible, is with a degree of coop-
eration and mutual help. I do not know whether a socialist system is the answer,
but I can say that the system that I see operating now is soulless and cold and
lacks human feeling and connection. I do not think most people want it this way
or like it, but I think the present capitalist model has brought this about. Perhaps
a better way to analyze this issue is that there should be other thought systems
and values than merely earning money. Money is necessary for all of us. Its purpose is not for us to enrich ourselves and devote ourselves to ourselves, but I
think it could be used as a great tool on behalf of others perhaps less fortunate
than ourselves.

A raw-edged capitalist system such as presently exists in the United States
makes us robots without feeling and without thought other than for ourselves. I

think the present system, as it exists, results in divisiveness, separation, and even alienation. It is significant to me that people feel the need to go online to find simple friendship and human companionship. It should be within all of us to form relationships and friendships that should be part and parcel of all our lives. I think the capitalist system in the Unites States, in its harshness and coldness, makes authentic human relationships virtually impossible, or at least hard and difficult. This is due to the system's creating in all our minds that we must get more and more and outdo more people around us, thereby not bringing about, if you will, a loving society. Rather what is created is society where people have no souls, or at least they cannot express to others what is in them or what they are capable of.

Chapter 59
Another Reason for Discrimination Law

At the present time in the United States, there are some few available legal remedies for the employee who perceives he has been unfairly treated by his employer, whether in being denied the position he has applied for, in not being promoted, in being terminated or in being subject over a lengthy period of time to a consistent pattern of harassment constituting a hostile work environment. There are a number of federal statutes that protect these employees from discriminatory actions on the part of the employer in the respects I have just mentioned. These include discrimination on the basis of disability, 42 USC Section § 12112 (Disability Discrimination); age discrimination, prohibited under 29 USC Section § 623; and discrimination based on national origin, race, sex, gender, and religion (42 USC Section § 2000e). There is also a state statute under Section 296 of the New York State Executive Law which prohibits discrimination on the basis of age, race, creed, color, national origin, sex, disability, or marital status.

All these statutes provide a remedy for the employee who has been discharged, refused a job, not promoted, or subjected to a hostile work environment if the employee can prove actual discrimination in these actions by the employer. These statutes are particularly important and significant in today's society. For some time now, unions have shrunk in numbers and power in the United States. As a result, few workers have the protection of any union from demotion, firing or, in general, unfair treatment on the part of their employer. Thus, most employees, unless they have civil service protection, have no job security.

This is particularly prevalent in the private sector, where most people are employed in the United States and where they can be terminated by their employer for virtually any reason at all. This is known as termination at will. Unless legislation is passed mandating that the employer provide some sort of job security, the employee has no other recourse but to sue under one of the discrimination statutes, if they can prove discrimination.

The capitalist system in this country which allows the employer to fire for any reason, except if discrimination can be proved, is not likely to be changed at any time in the near future. The present system, where firings occur on an extremely regular basis, makes life extremely difficult for the worker who needs a regular job to pay the expenses of maintaining his or her home or family. Thus, at the present point of time in society, these statutes have great importance and significance. They are the only way that provides any form of balance of power between employer and employee. Where there is a union or civil service protection, the employee is given the ability to defend himself against unfair treatment by the employer. The alternative is treatment that is completely outrageous and unfair on the part of the employer because the employer has such far and wide-raging discretion. Many times this discretion can take the form of discharging someone even for reasons of personal dislike or on the basis of personal chemistry and feelings by the employer. It is obvious that to discharge someone who has been doing their work competently because of personal dislike is not fair. The only break in our present society against these sorts of events and actions are these statutes. Until our present capitalist system can to some extent be altered and modified to allow the employees to keep their jobs, if they are doing their jobs, the employee's only weapon or recourse against a system that virtually eliminates the employee's ability to get a job, and certainly keep a job for any period of time, is these statutes.

In our present society, a situation has been created, or rather evolved, so that not only is the worker unable to keep his job for any period of time but he is not even allowed to earn a pension or have any long term benefits. These statutes may and have been abused by plaintiff employees who really have not been discriminated against but merely discharged for another reason, perhaps personal, on the part of the employer. I suggest, however, that under these statutes the courts of this country give the employee every chance to have some ability to survive in an economic system where they have been made pawns on a checker board and can be moved at will out of the economic system. The capitalist system cannot endure unless workers are given the right to have a job to pay their expenses and support their families. Without this, although the wealthy and management class may be enriched temporarily, the system will eventually fail and fall. I argue that these statutes are extremely critical and that the employee who brings suit under these statutes should be given every opportunity to present his case, since this is his or her only recourse in our present society. These statutes, in fact, may be the only way that our broad citizenry may be able to survive in a system where they are continually pushed farther and farther down, solely for the purpose and the enrichment of the corporate or wealthy class.

Chapter 60
A Society and Culture in Crisis

At the present time, our society and culture are in a spiritual crisis. There are many factors that, I think, have resulted in this situation. One factor is that the society is intensely, to some degree, secular. This means that people are concerned with advancing themselves and functioning in the society and world that they find presently before them. Most people may focus on having a sufficient material goods, having more money, or at least sufficient money, so that they can enjoy their lives to the fullest extent possible. Thus, one might say that religious belief or, better put taking account of a world outside of ourselves or a supernatural realm, is not societally connected to the extent is was formerly. Perhaps, one may say that the church, or religion in general, has less and less influence on people and their lives, at least in the West. It should be noted that religion still has great influence in Africa, most parts of Asia, the Middle East, and Arab countries. I am told that the number of Christians in China, for example, is growing greatly, and there has been great church growth in Africa as well.

It is also obvious that the emphasis on money and secularism in our culture has come to define people's wishes and desires greatly. The second factor in what I think is a spiritual crisis is technology: cell phones, computers, television, and our image culture in general. I think that these technological advancements, although good in many ways, divide people from one another and set up walls and boundaries. The result of this technology and the increased emphasis on materialism and the secular world view have brought about a kind of emptiness in people's lives. A life devoted to self, money, personal advancement, and a focus on technology creates walls and divisions.

I often hear people say, about others and even about culture and ideas, that they have no interest or concern or do not care. What is meant here is that our society has been directed to self alone and all other forces have been decimated and cut out. More exactly put, when we are only concerned with self, technology, and personal aggrandizement, the result will be that love in any form is cast out the window. Perhaps, one could more specifically state that when God or Christ is absent from a system which is only concerned with self-love, there can be no love. Jesus makes an unequivocal demand on all of us that we love our neighbor as ourselves. He commands us because he first loved us, his children and creation, and that love is unconditional.

In the absence of God and Christ and the rejection of the possibility of any spiritual or supernatural realm, we will always be divided as persons from one another, functioning in a sort of individual, capsulated, cold alienation. The increasing isolation, coldness, alienation and individual self-involvement will create a society of walled-off robots, incapable of feeling, of expressing feeling, or—most of all—of giving and receiving love. The price of the prosperity and wealth that we so desperately want will be a loveless, stale, and unforgiving society. In the absence of God and Christ, this is the prospect that we will all face.

Index of Specific Biblical References

Topical Index